ENDORSEMENTS

The thoughts in this book are urgent, practical, critically important, and vital. We have no choice if we want a bright future. Ron Luce explains what we need to do and why we need to do it. Packed into these pages are years of ministry experience and research. The result is an informative, hands-on guide for parents, pastors, and any adult looking to empower young people. I strongly encourage you to glean from Ron's wisdom the tools necessary to grow your church, impact your city, and transform a generation.

Ted Haggard
President, National Association of Evangelicals

As a parent of six children, I am very cognizant of the impact of media and entertainment on our kids. In *Battle Cry for a Generation*, Ron Luce takes the first important step: educating and equipping parents like me. It's our job to take the next step, parenting our children and helping them navigate the culturally hostile world that they and their peers live in twenty-four hours a day.

U. S. Senator Rick Santorum

Ron Luce effectively illuminates the plight of today's youth in our permissive culture ... This is a crisis in the making that we all need to be concerned about, and work together to avert.

Sean Hannity
Host, "The Sean Hannity Show" (ABC Radio)
and "Hannity & Colmes" (Fox News Channel)

The Bible tells us there is no retirement in war! In war, the time is crucial, the cost is great, but the cause is worth it! Our nation is in grave danger. The battle wages for the hearts and minds of the next generation. How I pray you'll not only read *Battle Cry for a Generation,* but that you'll join us on the front lines. I'm right there beside Ron Luce and Teen Mania, calling, "Be holy, even as He is holy."

Kay Arthur
CEO and Co-Founder
Precept Ministries International

It is the story of history that God uses the younger generation to revive and restore a nation that has fallen away (David, Daniel, Samuel, etc.). Therefore, the enemy often works to destroy youth before they can fulfill that destiny (e.g., the eradication of children by Pharaoh or Herod to destroy Moses and Jesus). It is no surprise, then, that today's cultural terrorists have targeted youth for spiritual destruction (through music, entertainment, education, technology, etc.). In this excellent work, Ron Luce has exposed the cultural terrorist "sleeper cells" at work within the nation, sounded a clarion alert, and set forth a succinct battle plan to defeat the enemy. Those who wish to see America retain her greatness must read this book.

David Barton
President, Wallbuilders

As someone who works with youth, I know how important it is to support them and do all we can to reaffirm who they are as unique persons created for a specific purpose by God. *Battle Cry for a Generation* is a call for all of us to be a part of this vital task.

Kirk Franklin
Grammy Award-winning Gospel artist and music minister

In a world that seems to be tumbling from crisis to crisis, there may be no more critical battle than for the hearts of our youth. With passion and vision from the front lines of this battle, Ron shares a battle cry for action.

Dr. David Ferguson
Executive Director, Intimate Life Ministries

Ron Luce knows the challenges teens face every day. *Battle Cry for a Generation* is a wake-up call for all of us who have a role to play in saving America's youth.

Josh McDowell
Author and speaker

For us who lead in America's church, it's too late for a mere "wake-up call" regarding the socio-spiritual crisis with today's youth-generation. Rather, it's time for a spiritual explosion that begets an aggressive, passionate leadership response to take action too long overdue. Ron Luce's book *Battle Cry for a Generation* is the powder keg that will propel discerning pastors and church leaders toward that response. I urge you—read it, let the fuse be lighted!

Jack W. Hayford
Founding Pastor, The Church On The Way
President, Foursquare Church International

Norman Schwarzkopf. Colin Powell. Tommy Franks. I read each of their books because they were on the front lines. And I read *Battle Cry for a Generation* for the same reason. I know of no one who has been more on the front lines in reaching this generation than Ron Luce.

Dr. Jay Strack
President, Student Leadership University

As a pregnant mother is responsible for the welfare and health of the child she carries, so is every nation responsible for the generation within its national womb. In this powerful, practical, profoundly passionate book, Ron Luce captures the urgency and danger of the critical state our youth are in and sounds a clear call to all who dare to accept the mandate to save a generation. This is a must read for the responsible heart.

Dr. Myles E. Munroe
President, Bahamas Faith Ministries International
Nassau, Bahamas

Ron Luce, to my mind, is the premier evangelist to the youth of America. In his new book *Battle Cry for a Generation*, Ron Luce issues a focused, clarion call for the leaders of our churches, and our homes, to rally to the front lines of the current cultural conflict and to fight fearlessly for the futures of our children.

His book lays out a clear and concise case for where we really are, and where we are really going—but what I really enjoyed was that he does not simply dwell in the realm of diagnosis, as many have before, but pushes on into the area of prognosis and gives us clear instructions on how we can effect a rescue. **This book is a must read for any leader who is interested in not seeing the baton of Christianity fall to the ground in this next generation!**

Rev. Chris Hill
President, CHM International

Ron Luce's *Battle Cry for a Generation* sounds the alarm on behalf of the youth of our time. Sharing surveys and statistics, Ron illuminates the attack of our culture on the teens of our nation. With practical suggestions, he encourages us to capture the heart of our present generation, thus insuring the moral fiber of our nation's future. Will you answer the cry?

Joyce Meyer
Best-selling author and Bible teacher

Ron Luce has written a compelling manifesto for every Christian parent and church leader. We are in a war with the most sophisticated enemy the church has ever faced, and the prize Satan hopes to claim is our own precious kids. It is time for us to adopt a wartime mentality and wise up to the subtle attacks that are taking place every day in our schools.

Willie George
Founder, Oneighty

Ron Luce communicates in a way that is compelling, convicting, and caring. He is a warrior, fighting the good fight for our generation and the generation to come. I am grateful that he calls us all to the battle to change America and the world by reaching our youth with the message of Jesus.

Dr. Jack Graham
Pastor, Prestonwood Baptist Church

What could be important than LEADING the next generation of LEADERS? Before we can do this, however, we have to understand both the gravity of the challenge and the promise of the opportunity. Make no mistake, this is a high-stakes game and *Battle Cry for a Generation* is a call to arms for anyone interested in our future. Where do I sign up?

Scott A. Snook
Associate Professor of Organizational Behavior
Harvard Business School

In *Battle Cry*, Ron Luce presents a frightening portrait on the effects of graphic violence and sexual images on the youth of our nation. But he also offers a message of hope if we who have a voice are willing to stand up and make a difference. Every parent of a teenager should read this book and take its important message to heart.

Edwin Meese, III
Former Attorney General

BATTLE CRY FOR A GENERATION

THE FIGHT TO SAVE AMERICA'S YOUTH

RON LUCE

BATTLE CRY FOR A GENERATION

THE FIGHT TO SAVE AMERICA'S YOUTH

RON LUCE

NE✚GEN®

Building the New Generation of Believers

COOK COMMUNICATIONS MINISTRIES
Colorado Springs, Colorado • Paris, Ontario
KINGSWAY COMMUNICATIONS LTD
Eastbourne, England

NexGen® is an imprint of
Cook Communications Ministries, Colorado Springs, CO 80918
Cook Communications, Paris, Ontario
Kingsway Communications, Eastbourne, England

BATTLE CRY FOR A GENERATION
© 2005 by Ron Luce

First printing 2005
Printed in Canada
                    3 4 5 6 7 8 9 10 Printing/Year 09 08 07 06 05

Cover Design: Brand Navigation, LLC
Interior Design: Sandy Flewelling

Teen photos are stock photos and not actual photos of the teens quoted in the
book.

All Scripture quotations, unless otherwise noted, are taken from the HOLY BIBLE,
NEW INTERNATIONAL VERSION®. Copyright © 1973, 1978, 1984 by International
Bible Society. Used by permission of Zondervan Publishing House. All rights
reserved.

ISBN: 0-78144-227-3

DEDICATION

To those in this generation
who are waiting to be reached
by each one who dares
to read this book.

ACKNOWLEDGMENTS

This work is a compilation of discoveries from the mentors who have guided me and the co-laborers who have ministered with me for the past 18 years.

I am grateful to Evie Reynolds, Casey Johnson, Juliana Diaz, and Beth Powell for the leadership in my office that has helped produce this book. Many thanks to Milana Dwire, Lorena Winger, Amanda Garza, Catherine Hicks, Christina Miller, Kristin Jessee, Francie Harrell, and Michal Price for their help in gathering and sorting research. Thanks also to Chad Arnold and Nate Dame for their tireless research on this project, and Dr. Judith Reisman for supplying some of the data used in the book. Mike Guzzardo and Joel Johnson, thank you for helping me take the message of this book to this generation.

I would really have no possible way of reaching this generation for Jesus Christ without the continual support and sacrifice of those on my leadership team at Teen Mania Ministries—Dave and Beth Hasz, D'Anne and Dennis Behee, Kevin and Wynne Benson, Rod and Michelle Arnold, Jon and Kelly Hasz, Dave and Linda Neal, Jon and Kim Taylor, and Rich and Kim Fuller. Their love for God and giving of their lives for the Cause have made this ministry possible and this moment a reality.

I want to thank Janet Lee and Gary Wilde for all their mercy and grace in working with me on this book. Sonia Weston, Kerry Park, Ted Ehrlichman, Dick Frieg, and the whole Cook family are amazing partners, as committed to rescuing this generation as we are.

I want to acknowledge all the staff at Teen Mania who labor tirelessly without limelight because of their love for Jesus and those who don't yet know Him. I am humbled that you are pouring so much into reaching those you have never met. I am unworthy of the devotion you show every day to this vision. Former staff and Lead Team members cannot be overlooked as true foundation stones that have helped make this moment possible.

The interns in the Teen Mania Honor Academy, past and present, must be recognized as those who are passionately committed to reaching their generation. Your reckless abandon to the call is exactly what it is going to take to bring your generation to faith in Christ. I am humbled and inspired at your dedication and I know that without you there would be far less fruit in the kingdom.

I have to acknowledge the Board members of Teen Mania Ministries: Daniel Williams, Jack Hayford, Lisa Robertson, Peter Lowe, George Babbes, and Myles Munroe. I don't know where I would be without your love and commitment to this generation, and I can't thank you enough. The mentors who have helped me become who I am are plentiful. I only wish I could have learned more quickly what you have taught through your lives and wisdom.

I want to thank my amazing children, Hannah, Charity, and Cameron. You all keep giving me a reason to keep coming home. Thank you for sharing me with the rest of your generation. Katie, my wife of more than 20 years, you are my foundation, my stability, my joy, and my best friend. This book would never be if you had not started this adventure with me and walked with me, heart and soul, every step of the way. There would be nothing to write had you not been fully engaged.

And finally, my God, what can I say to thank You? You changed my life and I only want that thing You did to me to happen to a whole generation. I know You want it even more, so may this book serve to further Your purpose to do so. My whole life is an expression of thanks to You for forgiving a debt I could never repay.

CONTENTS

F O R E W O R D

MEETING THE NEED FOR TRUTH

In the fall of 2003, I spoke at one of the most exciting events I've ever attended. It was a conference in Indianapolis organized by Teen Mania, a group founded by youth evangelist Ron Luce. Over three thousand youth ministers were in attendance. My subject: How to teach a Christian worldview to teenagers and prepare them to defend their faith in college.

The response was terrific. The youth ministers got it. They seemed to understand the importance of teaching worldview to kids. Instead of merely sharing the basics of faith, or just communicating a faith based mostly on good feelings, they understood that their task is to show kids a whole new way of looking at the world—a way that's radically different from the moral relativism that contemporary culture teaches them. These youth pastors can provide honest, intelligent, biblically-grounded answers to the serious questions many of these kids are asking.

Let me tell you, there's a desperate need for youth workers, educators, and parents who will do exactly this. In a recent survey, pollster George Barna reported that 83 percent of teenagers in this country today believe that "moral truth depends on the circumstances." Think about that. And "only 6 percent believe that moral truth is absolute." Perhaps most disturbing of all, "only 9 percent of born-again teens believe in moral absolutes." That's only one in ten of our Christian kids.

I can't think of a more urgent need than enabling young people to understand their faith and preparing them to defend it against the onslaught of secular thought they encounter in their schools and in popular culture.

The sad truth is that these kids don't understand what they say they believe about God, and they have no idea how their faith should affect their thinking and their lives. That's frightening not only for them, but also for the Church. If our future leaders don't believe in absolute truth—even though they say they know the God who is the source of all truth—what kind of future can we expect?

But the encouraging news is that the kids are asking the right questions. And in growing numbers, as I saw in Indianapolis, adults are lining up, ready to teach kids about worldview. Of special encouragement to me is that Teen Mania runs a worldview course at its Honor Academy based on the book Nancy Pearcey and I wrote called *How Now Shall We Live?*. It's an excellent one-year course that students take between high school and college.

This effort to teach Christian worldview to our youth has become a passion for me as it is for Ron Luce. I hope as you go through these pages it will become your passion, as well. Reading this book is the perfect place to begin. Teen Mania is a great ministry. Ron Luce is a gifted and capable leader. I wholeheartedly commend Ron and his writings to you.

In Ephesians, we're told that we are to work toward "the equipping of the saints for the work of the ministry." Clearly, given the corroded state of our culture, we cannot start too soon.

Charles W. Colson

today is d-day

The Allied invasion of Normandy became the turning point of World War II. Against formidable odds, nations came together to fight off evil—to win a war that once seemed un-winnable and to secure freedom for future generations.

Today we face our own D-Day. Now is the time for us to come together to win a war for this generation of young people. We have the chance of a lifetime to preserve for the children of America a future of freedom and promise. In this book, I will sound the alarm and the call to battle. I will share with you information and challenge you to action. This is a war for the heart and soul of a generation that we can win, if we *all* take action.

WHEN INACTION HURTS

The Nazis had stormed across Europe, pillaging and destroying the people and the land. They were determined to impose their ideology and values on the world and they had conquered virtually every nation they desired. Even as they threatened England with total domination, they seemed indestructible. Yet plans were being laid for a strategic counteroffensive.

The best minds in the free world had put nearly two years into the planning of the D-Day invasion. Still, everyone knew it could easily fail. None of the leaders felt secure or lived without worry. They knew the conflict would leave many children fatherless. They also knew that, even after losing many lives, the whole plan could still prove futile. It might only stir up a more ruthless Hitler.

Europe's volatile weather played an important role. If it rained just a little longer or harder, the whole thing would have to be called off. If the counterintelligence was unreliable, thousands of soldiers could walk right into a trap. Allied commanders had leaked false information to the Nazis to make them think the invasion would come from another region. But did they take the bait?

Yes, the generals knew there was great risk to their plan, but they knew there was *greater risk if they did nothing*.

The sad truth is that for several years England had been pleading with the United States to join the war effort. We had watched Hitler and his throngs of uniformed butchers annihilate nation after nation. Yet we remained inactive, a nation isolated and satisfyingly self-sustaining. For a long time, the horrifying pictures and stories from the war failed to provoke a response that could have saved many lives.

England continued to implore us to get involved. After all, they said, this war would eventually come right to our own homes, if we didn't soon wake up to the danger. They asked for money and troops. When Britain's Prime Minister Winston Churchill addressed a joint session of Congress in his famous speech—when everyone knew he was going to ask for money—he opened his remarks unexpectedly. He said to the senators and congressmen: "I did not come to ask for money ... (a long pause here and sustained applause from the joint session) ...*for myself*." Another pause. And then those final two words were answered with sustained applause that indicated he had succeeded in getting Americans to think about the terrible predicament confronting the people of Europe.

Churchill had called America to admit to its self-centeredness. He helped us realize there is something more important then self-interest. Americans began to understand that our future fate was tied to the current fate of others. We got involved but we still did not send troops. It would take the enemy blowing down our own back door at Pearl Harbor to summon forth our warriors.

ACTION SAVES LIVES

It's been said that the parents of the Baby Boomers are "the greatest generation." Having endured the Dust Bowl, the Great Depression, and World War II—and pressing through all the other hardships to preserve our nation—they deserve the title. We are enjoying quality life in America today won by their sacrifice.

One thing that made them so great was how they rallied together as a nation to meet a deadly foe. It seemed *everyone* took ownership during World War II. The men went to war, and the women went to work! People lived on rations and paid whatever price necessary to win that war. "We can do it" was their motto.

I hope that you'll see the great need for a similar kind of rallying as you learn about the ravages of the war being waged upon our teens. Today our adults must also arise. Though the weaponry is different, our war is just as fierce. It will require the same level of sacrifice, the same grim resolve. And no one is exempt of involvement if we mean to have victory. Every father, mother, businessman, grandparent, pastor, and youth pastor must hear the call.

Why do I begin by speaking of war? Because I have seen the enemies of our children march across the land, leaving ravished young hearts and minds in their wake. I have seen the wounding effects. I've listened to the stories of teens hurting, broken, and bleeding (some by their own hands). I've seen the signs of war, and you have too. Yet to no avail. Too few of us have taken action. Too few seem to realize that the enemy really is at our own back door.

It is time for us to wake up and acknowledge that this is our war for the hearts of today's teens and for the future of America. It is time now for us to get involved, not only as supporters but as warriors.

THE FACE OF THE ENEMY

Most of us had never heard the name "Al-Qaeda" before President Bush described the terrorist group in his post 9/11 address to Congress. He told us of its founder, Osama Bin Laden, who has since become a household name. We learned the group was well-funded and had established "sleeper cells" all over the world. It dawned on us that this newly revealed enemy was very smart and quite sophisticated. These certainly weren't simple-minded people living in the desert with a few machine guns.

Clearly, we would need to get to the center of the power structure, because the future of our nation depended on it.

That is also the case with the enemy who plots against our young ones—the techno-terrorists, the virtue-terrorists. They are terrorists of a different kind, but they are terrorists just the same. Here's why:

They are deeply funded and thoroughly organized. Like Al-Qaeda, they have money and they have plans. These enemies don't just promote violence on the silver screen; they are various entities with various motives. They use their technology and marketing arsenal to create and/or allow the culture of destruction to thrive happily among our teens. Certainly the entertainment media is the dominant form of influence and thus a huge culprit.

Consider MTV, whose parent company, Viacom, recorded revenues of $6.84 billion in 2004[1]. While MTV would never say its chief aim is to "destroy a generation," it is in fact doing that by seeking to make money off young people, no matter what it takes. The company has organized a "cradle to grave" program for your kids. It starts with Nickelodeon, then Nick Jr., both of which are owned by Viacom. These networks begin to train small children as to what is cool and what they should want to look like. They introduce them to pop icons and get them wanting their music and action figures. By the time the kids are interested in music videos, MTV presents a whole new world for them to "enjoy."

They are subversive and effective in promoting their agenda. These enemies of decency are already in our "nicest" families, as you'll soon see. Yes, even in the best of Christian homes. They've crashed through the gates, pushed down the door, and landed on the living room couch. Psalm 1:1 says "Blessed is the [person] who does not walk in the counsel of the wicked." We have a generation that isn't "blessed" because it has allowed the wicked to shape its values for life.

Many Christian parents are shell-shocked:

"How could my little girl end up pregnant?"

"Why are our kids using such language?"

"I thought I taught my son better than that. Why is he getting drunk all the time?"

"How could she wear something so skimpy to a party? That's not how I raised her!"

Maybe *you* did not raise her after all. Maybe the kids are exact replicas of the terrorists who actually raised them. Considering the proportion of time your kids spend "under the influence" of the virtue-terrorists, why are you surprised? The world has kidnapped our kids right under our noses. We have invited the terrorists into our homes and paid them to corrupt our kids. And considering the fact that 88 percent of kids raised in Christian homes do not continue to follow the Lord after they graduate from high school, it looks like the terrorists are winning.

A CALL TO ACTION

As you read through this book, you'll see a battle plan unfolding, a strategy that calls for your personal, dedicated involvement. I want you to see its basic outlines up front so that, as you read each chapter, you can constantly think about finding your personal assignment, or mission. This is not a casual suggestion. This is a serious call to arms. As the dire plight of our young people hits you in the pages to come, I believe you'll truly want to become heavily involved in this war. You'll want to find an assignment that demands your all and pushes you to reach out to young people who are being destroyed in the fray. So here is a summary of how you can enter the battle. There are two parts to the battle plan:

1. The National Campaign

☐ Go online at **www.battlecry.com** and enlist today in the Battle Cry Coalition to receive regular e-mail updates on exactly how to pray and stay involved in practical ways of reaching out to this generation.

☐ Voice your opinion now about how this generation is being bombarded with sexual images, telling stories that have happened in your family or community that demonstrate how this infection is hurting our teens.

2. The Front Lines

☐ Find a group of people (Sunday school class, Bible study, home group, or group of Christians at work) to go through this book with you. There's power in numbers: inspire others to get committed to this generation with you.

- Give a copy of this book to your pastor and youth pastor. Follow up with them once they have read it. Brainstorm together: What steps can you all take as a church to reach out to teens in your community?
- Talk to your local youth pastor/leader to find out how your gifts can be used to expand the youth ministry.
- If you have no youth leader in your church, make an appointment with your pastor right away—and volunteer for the job! Feel free to contact us at **www.teenmania.org** for all kinds of practical tools on what to do with the teens in your group to build them into an army for God.
- Find ways to invest financially into youth ministry, either locally or nationally. Research youth ministries that are making an impact on teens. Then give!

Finding your assignment is crucial. As you read this book, keep asking yourself: What is touching my heart right now? What need can I meet? What interests do I have? What gift can I use? Remember: Real lives are waiting on the other side of your obedience.

Stop right now and look over the above lists. Check which actions intrigue you even now. Everyone can do something. Plan time into your schedule now so you'll be ready for action as you become motivated by the things you'll learn in the coming pages. Come back to these lists frequently as you read each chapter.

For all the practical ideas mentioned in this book, there are a thousand more ways to enlist your energies in this cause. If you cannot find someone to join up with in the battle for a generation, start a brand-new movement in your area. Rally other parents and leaders in your town. Don't accept no for an answer. If you have never been involved in youth ministry before, start now. Then go get all your friends. It will take *all* of us.

Everyone is invited; everyone is required. "We must do better than our best. We must do whatever is required to win." These were Winston Churchill's words as he faced a determined enemy head-on. It is also the battle cry for a generation today.

Ron Luce
Spring 2005

---

[1] Associated Press, "Update 2: Viacom 2Q Results Rise on Cable, TV" on the Web at **www.Forbes.com /07/22/04, 10:47 AM**

time to wake up

Just as the events of September 11, 2001 permanently changed our perspective on the world, so we ought to be awakened to the alarming influence of today's culture terrorists. They are wealthy, they are smart, and they are real.

When President Bush declared war on international terrorists, he recognized that the *risks of underreacting were greater that the risks of overreacting*. Now we face the same reality.

CHAPTER ONE

the car's on fire

Chances are you didn't wake up this morning and decide, "Today, I'll be a hero." Opportunities for acts of heroism rarely show up on weekly planners or "To Do" lists. Instead, they intrude into everyday life, demanding split-second choices at great personal risk. At least that's the way it happened for my brother Ralph. One Sunday morning in the summer of 1998, Ralph steered his car out of the congested, post-service church parking lot. In the car ahead of him were two teenage girls. About a mile down the road, the girls halted their vehicle at a four-way stop, then proceeded carefully into the intersection as Ralph, his own car packed full with his wife and five small children, waited his turn to follow.

Without warning, a pickup truck sped through the intersection and slammed broadside into the car containing the two teenage girls. Ralph watched in disbelief as the driver, 17-year-old Ashley, was thrown from the car and killed instantly. His disbelief turned to horror as the car burst into flames, trapping the unconscious 14-year-old

I NEED PRAYER. I am really struggling a LOT right now. Since I was about six my dad has verbally abused me, and on occasion physically. When I was twelve, my great-grandfather started molesting me. And then seventeen days ago . . . this hurts me the most, I was raped when I was leaving work. I feel so dirty and used and abused and ashamed and I don't know what else. I feel like I'll never be clean. I have so much hatred in my heart right now. I hate my life. I want to kill myself to get away from the pain! It hurts! I can't handle it anymore! PLEASE HELP! — *Anonymous*

Amy inside. Ralph was suddenly out of his car and racing toward the burning vehicle. Somehow he managed to pry open the car door and, grabbing the belt loops of the limp and helpless teenager, free Amy from the inferno. Soon after Ralph pulled Amy to safety, paramedics whisked her away to the hospital where she fully recovered.

Suddenly Ralph was the town hero. He had saved a girl's life! Congratulations began pouring in from all over town, including the mayor's office. The local paper featured an article about Ralph's selfless act. When I discovered what had happened, I called Ralph to express my amazement at his courage. I tried to imagine what had inspired this father of five to risk everything—his personal safety, his family, his life—for a girl he barely knew.

Finally I asked him the question that was eating at me: "What were you thinking? I mean, what was going through your mind as you approached that burning car?"

"You know, Ron," Ralph replied, "I didn't do anything that anyone else in my position wouldn't have done. I don't know how I did it. All

I know is that *when the car is on fire, you do whatever you have to do to get the girl out!"*

People, the car is on fire and the youth of America are trapped inside. Suicide, abortion, alcohol, drug abuse, and violence are fiery flames licking at the wreckage of many young lives. The stakes are staggering—we have in America today 33 million teenagers, the largest group of teens since World War II.[1] This generation of youth has the potential to impact our nation—economically, politically, spiritually—with every bit as much force as the Baby Boomers have. These young people are our sons and daughters, brothers and sisters, grandsons and granddaughters, nieces and nephews. They are the future of America. We've got to get them out—whatever it takes— we've got to get them out.

NATION AT A CROSSROADS

Our nation has the proud heritage of being founded on Christian principles; many of our founding fathers were godly men. For two centuries we have enjoyed a society that—while not thoroughly Christian—is based on many of the moral imperatives from Scripture. But as our population has fallen from core evangelical, Bible-based beliefs, so has our society in our desire to be a tolerant, inclusive society. There is no longer a potent majority that speaks out when traditional biblical values are violated. This fact alone bears serious reflection, but I fear our present reality is much worse.

It is well documented that the percentage of Bible-based believers has steadily decreased since the Builder generation, as reflected

whatever direction this new generation takes, so it will take the nation.

in the following table from the book *The Bridger Generation* by Thom S. Rainer:[2]

- *Builders (born 1927-1945): 65% Bible-based believers*
- *Boomers (born 1946-1964): 35% Bible-based believers*
- *Busters (born 1965-1983): 16% Bible-based believers*
- *Bridgers (or Millennials, born 1984 or later): 4% Bible-based believers*

Think about what this means. While many Americans today may call themselves "Christians," only four percent of Millennials affirm themselves as church-attending, Bible-believing Christians. If that statistic doesn't alarm you, it should. It should alarm us all. Why? For the answer, we can look at the legacy left by previous generations in today's culture.

DECLINE OF CHRISTIAN CULTURE

For as long as many of us can remember, we have known that when the Boomers hit a certain age, their sheer numbers would affect all of American society more than any other generation in modern times. Today's corporate, political, and religious leaders are the Baby Boomers. With only 35 percent firmly believing in Scripture, they have shaped our culture with the following results:

- *Morally corrupt films and television programs*
- *An increasingly perverted music industry*
- *The pornographic invasion of the Internet*
- *Civil initiatives promoting gay marriage*
- *Battles to remove the Ten Commandments from public buildings, and fights to take "under God" out of our Pledge of Allegiance*

If these are the struggles we face now, with 35 percent of the largest generation of Americans affirming a belief in Scripture, can you imagine what America will be like when today's teens become the next generation to dominate the population, with only 4 percent currently claiming to be Bible-believing Christians?

Seventy-one million Millennials (33 million now in their teens) hold our future in their hands. Our national destiny is linked to this new generation. Try to imagine a society that mocks the fact that "under God" was *ever even in* our Pledge of Allegiance. Try to imagine the motto "In God we trust" taken off our money. Imagine all references to Christ and His cross removed from all emblems and city logos. Try to imagine a world where a pastor can go to jail for saying homosexuality is wrong. Current news stories confirm that these unfortunate events are already happening here and in other nations around the world. If we think Christians are persecuted and marginalized now in the U.S., imagine being the laughingstock of society! Is this the price we must pay for neglecting to build a solid biblical framework into the hearts of our children and our children's children?

WHO WILL SAVE AMERICA'S YOUTH?

History is rich with examples of first-generation believers who paid a high price for their faith. That price was paid so future generations could thrive in a society with religious freedom. To those early believers, America was a "city on a hill," a nation set aside for God's purposes—a country established for good and fruitfully blessed so that we might take God's message to the ends of the earth.

I'M DROWNING

in my sea of blood, hate, and deception. I'm drowning ... dying. Does anybody care? — *Beth*

decades may pass before any other generation has the opportunity to effect change of this magnitude.

Whatever direction this new generation takes, so it will take the nation. We need not be left only to imagine the America of tomorrow. It is within our power, as Christian leaders, parents, and concerned adults, to shape the next generation of Americans. Together we can ensure that our children and our grandchildren grow up in a society fortified by biblical principles and a strong moral code. It is the heritage our forefathers fought and died to secure for us. Can we do less than fight for the same values for the next generation?

For over 18 years, I've regularly crisscrossed our country speaking to millions of representatives of this future generation. I am compelled to do so because of how Jesus radically saved and changed me when I was a 16 year old trapped in drug abuse and a broken home. Since then, He has given me the opportunity to share with millions of hurting teens how He alone has the power to heal their shattered lives. I have seen the worst of the worst as I travel and conduct Acquire the Fire conferences weekend after weekend—and I know that no one is beyond the reach of God's loving hand. But never before have I felt so compelled to sound an alarm, a call to take up arms in the battle of the new millennium.

This is our moment in history. Decades may pass before any other generation has the opportunity to effect change of this magnitude. The car is on fire. We see it burning and we know that there is someone trapped inside. *This crisis demands our response.* We've got to leave the comfort of our cars—our own families, churches, and communities—and take a risk. Will we prove we are ready for the challenge of our day? Will history condemn our apathy and self-indulgence and grieve that our moment passed without our resolute commitment to make a difference?

NOW IS THE TIME

A holy urgency burns in my soul to capture the heart of this generation NOW while teens are still open to the life-changing message of the Gospel of Christ. This is what keeps me awake at night. Today is our moment of greatest opportunity. We must capture their hearts while they are young. We have a short window of 5 to 7 years before most of them will be into their 20s and set the pace for American culture.

Our nation is truly at a crossroad. What we do in the next 5 years could affect the next 50 to 100 years of American history. Every year in America, 4.5 million teenagers turn 20 years old. Research shows that once a child reaches that milestone, the odds of reaching that individual for Christ are nearly 10 to 1. In fact, the Barna Research Group has gathered data that leads them to conclude that "what you believe by the time you are 13 is what you will die believing."[3]

Something is happening right in front of the faces of Christians here in America that demands our attention. It is not my intention to overwhelm you with data (although the statistics will alarm you) because this book is not about data; it is about our children. I want to give you just enough facts to help you get a clear picture of the situation so that you can begin to see what we can do as a force for God to rescue our dying teens.

These words of mine cannot serve as just another news flash. This book cannot be just another book that makes us concerned without provoking our commitment and sacrifice. This is not a time for "business as usual" in our outreach to teens. If we do not act now, in twenty years we will all look back and say, "If we had only known.

If we had only done something."

This is our moment, our defining moment. What we do now in this season will determine the next hundred years of American history. The actions we take now will determine whether or not America continues on her current path toward becoming a post-Christian nation or returns to her legacy as a nation under God. In the pages that follow, I intend to help you hear the anguished cries of millions of teens, to stir your hearts to action, and to present a plan for engaging in the battle for this generation.

In the next chapter I'll get even more specific about how we can know the enemy confronting us. For we cannot go back and pretend these acts of terror never happened. We can't go along with business as usual. And surely we will not allow the enemies of our offspring to quietly plot their destruction solely by our inaction. It's way past time to wake up.

---

1 U.S. Census Bureau.

2 Thom S. Rainer, *The Bridger Generation: America's Second Largest Generation, What They Believe, How to Reach Them* (Nashville, TN: Broadman & Holman Publishers, 1997).

3 Research Shows That Spiritual Maturity Process Should Start at a Young Age, The Barna Group, Ltd., November 17, 2003. **http://www.barna.org/FlexPage.aspx?Page=Barna Update&BarnaUpdateID=153**

CHAPTER TWO

know your enemy

A media tidal wave is drowning our kids.

Or think of it as a dam break. Imagine your child standing in front of Hoover Dam as a fault in the wall breaks open. Your precious 14 year old is swept away in a massive wall of water and debris, struggling, gasping for breath. You watch in horror, helpless to save her and wondering in your heart, "How did this happen? Who's to blame for this catastrophe?" But when you ask the authorities about this murderous flood, they blame *you*: "Why didn't you teach your child to swim better?"

Hollywood's producers constantly fire off the same kind of question: "Why didn't you teach your child to watch better?" They're the first to tell parents they must regulate what their kids see—and they're right. Even actresses like Jamie Lee Curtis, and directors like Steven Spielberg, severely restrict what their own children watch on television.

But in light of the media tsunami sweeping across our kids, parents and any concerned adults who are morally conscious are in light of the media tsunami sweeping across our kids, parents and any concerned adults who are morally conscious are confronted daily with overwhelming odds.

confronted daily by overwhelming odds. And what about the parents who are too busy to even care that the dam has burst? Shouldn't the rest of us take responsibility for their kids? Or should we just stand by and watch as they plunge downstream with the blast of water? What of the danger that the drowning victims might pull our own kids under with them?

"Well, their parents should have taught them to swim." Will that be our response, based on the dubious logic of those seeking to profit from their destructive creations? It's like drinking water from a fire hose. Imagine trying to help your child take one small sip from your healthy, moral water fountain while he's blasted in the face by polluted water from the hose. What would he fill up on?

History tells us that if we're to win a war then we must know our enemy well. The well-planned response to Hitler on D-Day flowed from a careful study of his tactics and tendencies. General Eisenhower and his cohorts predicted the Fuhrer's moves, fully recognizing the propensities of his German army. And Sun Zhu, in *The Art of War*, the classic war strategy manual read by every military strategist for hundreds of years, wrote of it: "If you know the enemy and know yourself, you need not fear the result of a hundred battles. If you know yourself but not the enemy, for every victory gained you will also suffer a defeat. If you know neither the enemy nor yourself, you will succumb in every battle."

HOW BAD IS IT?

We don't want to succumb, so we must begin studying this enemy closely. Everyone knows, of course, that there's a lot of bad stuff on television and on the Internet. But just how bad is it? Do you think you know? Take a glimpse into the teenage media world for a few minutes by really looking at four of the biggest influences.

Television and movies: *dripping with violence, sex, and alcohol.* Nearly 61 percent of all television programming contains violence, with children's programming being the most violent. A recent comprehensive analysis of rock music videos of all types showed that 22.4 percent of all MTV videos portrayed overt violence, 20 percent of all rap videos contained violence, and 25 percent of all music videos depicted weapon carrying. And since more than half of 16 year olds see the majority of the most popular R-rated movies, they and other teens view an estimated ten thousand acts of violence each year. [1]

Does this seem bad? Not for Hollywood. And they saturate it all with sex, as well. The so-called "family hour" contains more than eight sexual incidents per hour. Each year teens absorb nearly fifteen thousand sexual references, with less than 170 of them referring to abstinence, birth control, or sexually transmitted diseases. And a recent analysis showed that 70 percent of all prime-time programming depicted alcohol, tobacco, or illicit drug use.

In addition to regular television programming, our young people see about twenty thousand commercials each year, of which two thousand peddle beer and wine. For every rather drab anti-drug commercial they may stumble upon, they'll be thoroughly entertained by 25 to 50 clever beer and wine advertisements. The ad campaigns have got to be perfectly riveting, because alcohol manufacturers want their money's worth—they spend $2 billion annually luring our kids to drink up.

Who creates all this entertainment? Sociologists conducted a survey of 104 of Hollywood's elite, asking the most influential writers and producers a number of ideological questions. The findings showed:

- *93 percent seldom or never go to worship services;*
- *97 percent believe in a woman's right to abort;*
- *5 percent strongly agree that homosexuality is wrong;*
- *16 percent agree that adultery is wrong;*
- *99 percent believe that television should be "more critical" of Judeo-Christian values.*[2]

Nielsen Media Research tells us that one of the highest rated television shows among girls 12-17 years old is "Will and Grace," a show portraying two lead characters as homosexuals. For boys in the same age group, "The Simpsons" topped the list, and this program is famous for denigrating parental authority. Nielsen also estimates that 13.9 million kids ages 2-17 were watching the 2004 Super Bowl when Janet Jackson experienced her "wardrobe malfunction." And on December 10, 2003, over two million kids, ages 2-17, were watching the Billboard Music Awards when FOX failed to bleep out the f-word.[3]

Music: *pounding home the obscenities.* The enemy isn't limited to television and movie screens, of course. Going far beyond the limits of decorum and good taste—while foregoing any attempt at true musicality—most of today's hits simply dish up steaming helpings of vileness. Am I overstating the case? You be the judge as you sample a few typical lyrics:

- ***Title: Halie's Revenge, 2003***
  Artist: Eminem
  Do-ra-mi, but we don't sing m-f—
  So Murder Inc. do ya thing m-f—

Don't you never say my little girl's name in a song again!
F—in' punk p—sy little b—h!
I'll f— you up boy!
Never in your m-f—in' life!
I'll choke the s— outchu little m-f— b—h!
Hailie can whip your m-f— a—!

- ### Title: American Idiot, 2004
  ### Artist: Green Day
  Don't wanna be an American idiot.
  Don't want a nation that under the new media.
  And can you hear the sound of hysteria?
  The subliminal mindf— America

- ### Title: Play It Off, 2004
  ### Artist: Nelly
  I play it off 'til it's played out
  I had her m-f— a— on the couch, kinda laid out
  She hittin them—gettin ate out

- ### Title: She Don't Know My Name, 2004
  ### Artist: Nelly (featuring Snoop Dogg, Ron Isley)
  Hey girl, what's yo' fantasy?
  Can I take you home? I want you here with me.
  Ooh girl you blow my mind, I want to be yo' freak
  Let me take you there, to that ecstasy, hoo
  Ooooooooooooh ba-by, ba-by
  Gotta get you home with me tonight
  Oh oh oh oh ohhhhhhhh, what's your name?
  What's your name?
  Gotta get you home with me tonight dear

do you feel like taking a bath yet?

- *Title: F— That, 2004*
  Artist: Kidd Rock
  So let's ride, not slide, let's mack
  And if they say you can't go around her, say F— THAT
  So let's ride, not slide, let's mack
  And if they say you can't go around him say F— THAT

- *Title: You Never Met A Motherf— Quite Like Me,*
  2003
  Artist: Kidd Rock
  I'm home hey I'm home
  You never met a motherf— quite like me
  Not like me, dida dada like me, hey like me

- *Title: Hot in Herre, 2003*
  Artist: Nelly
  Its gettin hot in here (so hot)
  So take off all your clothes
  I am gettin so hot, I wanna take my clothes off

Talk about artistic genius. Do you feel like taking a bath yet? This is only a sample of what kids across the land hear thousands of times a day. In fact, some young people, including churchgoing teens, are virtually glued to a boom-box 24/7. How much of this do they need to hear before it affects their attitudes and behaviors?

Video games: *Encouraging deadly mayhem "fun."* In case you hadn't noticed, video games have come a long way from the harmless, hungry little Pac-Man. Today, the video game business is a $7 billion industry.⁴ These 3-D animated extravaganzas have become a surreal world of raunch and gore, exploiting the wild frontiers of teenage imagination. In most cases, players are actually rewarded for dreaming up robberies, killings, and effective ways to solicit prostitutes. In "Sims 2," you even get to play God. The ad for its newest version boasts: "The Sims provide DNA data and inherited physical personality traits which let you control your computerized offspring from birth to death. Groom future generations, direct your own Sims movies, or simply enjoy the fruits of life without the burden of human interaction."

Even though the worst games are rated M (for "mature"), teens still play them. These are some of the most popular games among our kids:

- *Grand Theft Auto: San Andreas*
  Rated M for Mature: Intense violence or language; may include mature sexual themes. Players become gangsters, getting their kicks by stealing cars. They can relieve the tension of killing other players' characters by hiring prostitutes to have sex with them in the cars. The sex is offscreen, but conveyed by ecstatic moaning, the car's rocking, and the vibration of the game pad.

- *Doom 3*
  Rated M for Mature: Intense violence or language; may include mature sexual themes. Players compete to dismember and dispatch zombies and other creatures by using chainsaws, guns, and grenade launchers.

- *Warhammer 40,000: Dawn of War*
  Rated M for Mature: Intense violence or language; may

include mature sexual themes. In this game, according to its advertising copy, "hundreds of units clash on the battlefields of the dark future, unleashing massive destruction through a stunning battery of long-range weaponry before closing in for the finish. Incredible kill animations bring science fiction combat to life ... provides a striking tableau for the chaos and carnage of this grim, dark future."

- **EverQuest II**
  Rated T for Teen: *May contain violent content, mild, or strong language, and/or suggestive themes. Players consult "The Tome of Destiny," an apparent scripture text that begins: "There is only one solution: Destroy them all." Teens will place themselves in a world of zombies, sirens, griffins, and succubuses while using ancient weapons for deadly combat.*

- **Half-Life 2**
  Rated M for Mature: *Gore, horror, and realistic violence. A non-stop blood fest rages amidst an alien invasion.*

- **Halo 2, Limited Edition**
  Rated M for mature: *Some blood and gore, language, and violence. Players must kill all their alien enemies, whose blood runs blue across the screen.*

- **Resident Evil: Outbreak**
  Rated M for Mature: *Gore, horror, and realistic violence. At the beginning comes a warning that the game contains "explicit violence and gore." As one of a few survivors who have not been turned into a zombie by a mutating virus, a player must use such weapons as butcher knives and Molotov cocktails to decimate the living dead.*

The Internet: *Downloading the pervasive hardcore.* First, realize a big problem: Surfing the Web cuts down on family time, according to a study by Stanford University. "We were very interested to discover that the increase in Internet use over the last 10 years has eaten into television viewing less than expected," said Norman Nie, director of the Stanford Institute for the Quantitative Study of Society. "Time online seems to come more out of family discretionary time." The researchers found that average Internet users spend three hours per day online, almost double the 1.7 hours watching television.[5]

And what are people doing online? According to the charted categories in the study, they are spending more time viewing "adult" Web sites than the time spent scheduling events, social networking, investigating politics, communicating by e-mail, doing personal banking, or searching for specific information.[6]

If this is what the average adult is doing, what are hormone-hounded teens likely to be doing online? Currently, there are over 300,000 pornographic Web sites for teens to explore on the Internet, according to David Burt of N2H2, and the number is growing every day. Perhaps this is why the National Center for Missing and Exploited Children found that one in five children ages 10-17, who regularly use the Internet, have received a sexual solicitation while online. One in four was unwillingly exposed to images of naked people or people having sex.[7]

A clever disguise operates here among the cascading floods of media influence on our young people. The Bible says in 2 Corinthians

one in five children ages 10-17, who regularly use the Internet, have received a sexual solicitation while online.

MY MOM AND DAD just got a separation. My mom is often leaving my little brother with me to go out with her friends. I asked her if I could go out and she said no because she said I would be doing drugs and drinking. But what she doesn't understand is if I wanted to I could drink and do drugs without going to parties. You see I used to live in Vegas and all I did was go to parties and drink and everything like that. I got raped by my ex-boyfriend last year and after that I started Cutting myself and I became bulimic. Now I don't know how to tell my mom cause she is bulimic too. So can you please pray for us. — *Zoe (15)*

11:14, "And no wonder, for Satan himself masquerades as an angel of light." In this case, he's disguised by the cool, the popular, the trendy themes the media tells us are the cultural norms. While very young, children begin hearing exactly what they should look like, act like, be like.

WHAT ARE THE EFFECTS?

Does this constant media barrage really affect our kids all that much? Not if you ask most producers. And, they say, they're only creating what people want to buy. They satisfy their consciences by explaining, "We're merely reflecting society as it is today" and "long before television there was violence." So how can we criticize any particular show or film?

However, the issue is not a particular program or video game. The real issue is the cumulative effect of an environment, an atmosphere that now overflows with sex and gore. Consider the power of this unending stream of perversity.

It glazes them. Ever been so fixed on the television screen that you were quite rude to a loved one who dared interrupt? You just didn't want to miss a single word! Many teens live, day in and day out, in this media-induced trance. Whether the source is movies, music, or the Internet, the addictive nature of the media can make our "real" lives and relationships fade into the background. It's easier to remain frozen in an escapist glaze than to face real problems, real people, or real boredom.

Perhaps that's why more families own a television set than a telephone. Young people take in over eighteen thousand hours of television by the time they graduate from high school—over five thousand more hours than they spend in their 12 years of classes. In fact, American children spend more time watching television than they spend on any other activity except sleeping.[8]

Young people average 16 to 17 hours per week watching television. If we add video games and video movies, we find that teenagers spend as many as 35 to 55 hours per week in front of a screen. Despite the hectic pace of the average home's daily activities, families still have time to tune into over 50 hours of television per week, which is 10 hours more than the normal work week. With this level of media consumption, is it possible that teens are left unaffected? Could they really imbibe all that sex and violence and somehow fail to be shaped by it?

whether the source
is movies, music, or the
Internet, the addictive nature
of the media can make our "real"
lives and relationships fade
into the background.

we now have a generation that seems to reflect the values of the media more than it reflects the values of its Christian parents.

It hazes them. After seeing and listening to so much bad stuff, here's what happens: Right and wrong become a little hazy. And since a teen's idea of what is important and valuable has been so diligently shaped by those with no absolutes, what would we expect? Yet God-fearing parents still wonder why their young girls come to them wanting to wear tight, skimpy clothes that show too much skin, or wonder where their young men could have learned such curse words. They find themselves in arguments with their own teens about why "homosexuality may not really be wrong after all, since people can't help it; they were born that way."

It's been said that musicians are today's modern-day philosophers. They shape the thinking of the masses, and when our kids listen to what the masses listen to, they become just like them. They enter the fuzzy, hazy world of moral relativism.

It raises them. We now have a generation that seems to reflect the values of the media more than it reflects the values of its Christian parents. Has the media actually done the job that we were supposed to do? And is this why polls by Barna and Gallup find that it is hard to see much difference between the lifestyles of Christian and non-Christian teens?

After all, Christian young people have been trained to admire the same people that their non-Christian peers look up to. They cheer for the same pop stars and movie stars that the worldly teens cheer for, no matter what those stars say and do. As long as these celebrities remain famous, they're deemed worthy of honor. And this is where the real problem lies. The principle of honor begins to show itself. You see, when we honor someone, we allow them to influence us and actually give them authority in our lives. People whom we truly admire . . .

> . . . we listen to, not wanting to miss a single word;
> . . . we go out of our way to support and serve;
> . . . we emulate, because we want to be just like them.

When teens find a musician they like, they often memorize every lyric on a CD and read every word of the musician's interviews. These kids go out of their way to buy a concert ticket, even if it means waiting up all night. Many young people start dressing like their favorite artists, even taking on their mannerisms.

Our problem is that too often, we in the church honor the same people the world does. No wonder our Christian teens look just like any other teen! We invite the world to come into our living rooms and teach our kids who is honorable. As a result, these immoral shapers of culture and media have been given the authority to shape a whole generation.

WHAT ABOUT THE RESEARCH?

Countless studies prove what I've been saying. For example, it's clear that there's no gene for violence; it is a learned behavior. *Over a thousand studies*, including a Surgeon General's report in 1972 and a National Institute of Mental Health report 10 years later, attest to more than a casual connection between media violence and aggressive behavior in some children. Such studies show that the more lifelike

no wonder our Christian teens look just like any other teen!

FOR THE PAST

couple of years people in my school have been telling me to kill myself. It has lowered my concentration and i ended up failing the class. Recently, my mother told me i'm nothing and i'm worthless—it slipped out while we were having a fight but she still said it and i always remember the times she's called me fat. i'm now bulimic and a self-mutilator. There are days i can't go through the day without cutting myself up to 30 times. i suffer from major depression and i do drugs. i used to be a Christian and i still consider myself one. i'm just no longer sure if I'm going to heaven or hell. i still go to church as much as i can and i only listen to Christian music but still i'm not sure. i'm not asking for prayer. Basically, i'm not worth that much. i just thought i could talk to you. — *Rachael*

the violence portrayed, the greater the likelihood it will be learned.[9] And a study of 1,792 teens ages 12-17 showed that watching sex on television influences teens to have sex. (Who on earth would have thought such a thing?) Now a brand-new study by the RAND Corporation, published in Pediatrics, shows beyond a doubt they are connected.[10]

One of the most obvious examples of the connection between media violence and teen behavior occurred on April 20, 1999. The two Colorado teens who killed 12 classmates at Columbine High School spent endless hours blasting make-believe opponents in violent video games, including the game Doom.

Real-life stories are plentiful, of course. But I'd like to share just a few more to illustrate the powerful influence of media and video games on our teens.

- In November 2002, an Ohio girl was beaten to death by a 15-year-old boy with one of the posts from the victim's bed. (Investigators later discovered that the boy's favorite way to kill in the video game Grand Theft Auto was to use a baseball bat.) The boy then stole her car, as players do in the game. Witnesses say the murderer played the game for hours, turning into a "zombie" when he played.[11]

- In Michigan, during the Christmas season of 2003, witnesses say three Grand Theft Auto 3 devotees played the game for hours, then hopped into their car and purposely ran over a man they didn't know (as players do in the game), went to breakfast, came back and stomped him into a coma (as players do in the game), and then went home and played the game some more.[12]

- On January 31, 2003, police in Oakland, California, arrested a group of young men, known as the "Nut Case" gang, for dozens of car jackings, robberies, and murders. Police say they were using Grand Theft Auto 3 to train for these crimes and to get fired up to do them. Said one perpetrator: "We played the game by day and lived the game by night."[13]

- In Ft. Lauderdale, Florida, on February 10, 2002, 17-year-old Gorman Roberts was accused of pushing 5-year-old Jordan Payne into a canal and letting him drown. Roberts walked away laughing and told police later that he, Payne, and a third child had watched a World Wrestling Entertainment we can't stand by and do nothing amidst this deluge of sounds and images—even if it means combating something as powerful as MTV and Hollywood.

program featuring The Rock three days before the incident. Roberts' attorney, Ellis Rubin, said, "Little boys imitate what they see on television. If they hadn't been watching wrestling, none of this might have happened."[14]

- On July 1, 2001, five pupils at a school in Oldham, Manchester, England, turned up with flesh wounds on their forearms after copying a scene from an Eminem video in which a disturbed fan is seen slitting his wrists. The children, as young as 10 years old, told teachers they had dismantled pencil sharpeners so they could use the blades to cut themselves.[15]

- A $246 million lawsuit was filed against the designer, marketer, and a retailer of the video game series Grand Theft Auto by the families of two people shot by teenagers (in Knoxville, Tennessee) who were apparently inspired by the game. The suit claims that marketer Sony Computer Entertainment America, Inc., designers Take-Two Interactive Software and Rockstar Games, and Wal-Mart are liable for $46 million in compensatory damages and $200 million in punitive damages. Aaron Hamel, 45, a registered nurse, was killed. Kimberly Bede, 19, of Moneta, Virginia, was seriously wounded when their cars were hit on June 25 by .22-caliber bullets as they passed through the Great Smoky Mountains. Stepbrothers William Buckner, 16, and Joshua Buckner, 14, of Newport, were sentenced in August to an indefinite term in state custody after pleading guilty in juvenile court to reckless homicide, endangerment, and assault. The boys told investigators they got the rifles from a locked room in their home and decided to randomly shoot at tractor-trailer rigs, just like players do in the video game Grand Theft Auto 3.[16]

WHAT CAN WE DO?

After all of this bad news, we may feel like throwing in the towel and giving up. But please realize that we can do much to reverse the situation—if only we'll act immediately with resolute determination.

First, there is the parental responsibility we have for our own children. In my family, we decided not to use television as a babysitter for our children. We have carefully guarded their total media intake for their whole lives so far. As a result they haven't become addicted to certain programs and haven't begged us for many of the toys filling their friends' bedrooms. They haven't longed to dress like Britney Spears, or any other pop star. In fact, they see through the veil that has been cast by much of the media.

Without a doubt, we, as parents, can and should guard what our own kids see and hear. We can follow the cues from both Hollywood's elite and the biblical mandate to guard their hearts. We must teach our kids to:

- *Set their minds on the things above rather than earthly things (Col. 3:2);*
- *Love what is pure; hate what is evil; cling to what is good (Rom. 12:9);*

- *Avoid letting the world teach them to love what is evil or to envy the evil doer (Prov. 24:1);*
- *Stay away from the bins shoveling "beautiful garbage" (Ps. 101:3).*

Second, we can reach out to the "sons and daughters of America" without parents who demonstrate such prudence. Why should we let the broken dam wash them away? Studies have shown, again and again, that religious beliefs and churchgoing can help them at many levels:

- *The strength of the family unit is intertwined with the practice of religion.*
- *Religious belief and practice contribute substantially to the formation of personal moral criteria and sound moral judgment.*
- *Regular religious practice generally inoculates individuals against a host of social problems, including suicide, drug abuse, out-of-wedlock births, crime, and divorce.*
- *The regular practice of religion encourages such beneficial effects on mental health as less depression (a modern epidemic), more self-esteem, and greater family and marital happiness.*
- *In repairing damage caused by alcoholism, drug addiction, and marital breakdown, religious belief and practice are a major source of strength and recovery.*
- *Regular practice of religion is good for personal physical health: It increases longevity, improves one's chances of recovery from illness, and lessens the incidence of many killer diseases.*[17]

Clearly, involvement in the Christian world really can save our teens from the tragic future awaiting them if they remain so thoroughly influenced by the dominant media. Therefore, we must find a way to reach out and pull them away from the media torrent rushing at them every day. We can't stand by and do nothing amidst this deluge of sounds and images—even if it means combating something as powerful as MTV or Hollywood.

In the Bible, Nehemiah told his builders to work with a tool in one hand and a sword in the other. Jesus called us to watch and pray. Let us pray first, and then take action.

Before Nehemiah took action, he carefully explored the damage done to the wall. He knew he needed to understand exactly what it would take to rebuild it. Like Nehemiah, we need to understand the extent of the damage to this generation. Lest this document seem like another rehashing of a "those kids really have it bad" mentality, let's dive in and look closely at the ugly truth. We live in a time where brand new forces are not only shaping our kids, but dominating the culture and pillaging our moral heritage from the next generation. This is no fake war.

1   To find statistics like these—and many others—go to such Web sites as:
    www.parentstv.org; **www.frc.org**; or **www.clickz.com/stats/sectors/demographics**.

2   For information about the most influential writers/producers, see: "Violence and Promiscuity
    Set the Stage for Television's Moral Collapse," Issue#: 248 **www.frc.org/get.cfm?i=IS02E4**.

3   See three Web sites: **http://www.parentstv.org/ptc/facts/mediafacts.asp**;
    http://www.newjerzee.com; **www.tvturnoff.org**.

4   Time Magazine, "Video Vigilantes," January 10, 2005.

5   Reported by Rob McGann in an article titled, "Internet Edges Out Family Time More than TV
    Time," January 5, 2005, at Web site: **www.clickz.com/stats/sectors/demographics/
    article.php/3455061**.

6   Rob McGann, Ibid.

7   Regarding the amount of porn sites and spam, see: National Coalition for the Protection of
    Children & Families **www.nationalcoalition.org/internetporn/internetporn.html**.

8   For statistics on how much television children are watching, see:
    http://www.tvturnoff.org/images/facts&figs/factsheets/FactsFigs.pdf.

9   Parent TV Council, p.4

10 See pages 22-23 of Report 6 article. Footnoted in that article to Family Pride Canada, Web
    site: **http://familypride.uwo.ca/teens/teenbk2.html**.

11 "Violent Videogames a Case for Legislation," by Valerie Smith. Submitted to the Canadian
    Association of Chiefs of Police and the Canadian Police Association, March 13, 2003.

12 "Violent Videogames a Case for Legislation," Ibid.

13 "Violent Videogames a Case for Legislation," Ibid.

14 "Monkey See, Monkey Do," p. 6 (Associated Press, 5/14/02).

15 "Monkey See, Monkey Do," p. 7 (BBC News Online, 7/13/01).

16 From a news story on CNN.com, "Lawsuit filed against Sony, Wal-Mart over game linked to
    shootings," 10/23/03.

17 See "The Impact of Religious Practice on Social Stability," on the Web at
    www.heritage.org/Research/Religion/BG1064.cfm.

CHAPTER THREE

this is a real war

In our battle for the current generation, we are losing ground—and we have little ammunition left. The enemy has pinned us against the wall, giving us scant hope of survival.

How did we land in this tight spot? We retreated here, giving up ground to the point of embarrassment. In the name of "freedom of speech" and "tolerance" we abdicated our responsibility to this young generation and to our nation's heritage. Now politically correct virtue-terrorists have mined the verbal landscape with convoluted logic, leaving us nearly powerless to protect our young ones. Teens are lying in our arms bleeding, gasping for their last breaths, and we pity them for having to deal with the deadly explosions. In fact, most of us are secretly relieved: "I'm so glad I didn't have to grow up with all of this going on."

The sad truth is that the words "war" and "battle" work as metaphors in this arena. We imagine the devil as a mean little guy running around in a red suit, enticing people to do naughty things.

this is not just a social war; it is a spiritual war.

Lulled into complacency by the illusion of his bothersome impish-ness, we stand by as he does serious damage—massacring our children's minds, hearts, and destinies.

This is not just a social war; it is a spiritual war. To face the enemy and to fight the battle, we must be spiritually strong and take on a thoroughly scriptural warrior mentality:

> *Praise be to the LORD my Rock, who trains my hands for war, my fingers for battle. —Psalm 144:1*

> *Fight the good fight of the faith. Take hold of the eternal life to which you were called when you made your good confes-sion in the presence of many witnesses. —1 Timothy 6:12*

> *Endure hardship with us like a good soldier of Christ Jesus. —2 Timothy 2:3*

> *Put on the full armor of God so that you can take your stand against the devil's schemes. —Ephesians 6:11*

> *The weapons we fight with are not the weapons of the world. On the contrary, they have divine power to demolish strong-holds. —2 Corinthians 10:4*

Jesus Himself exhorts us to engage in the battle: "From the days of John the Baptist until now, the kingdom of heaven has been force-fully advancing, and forceful men lay hold of it" (Matt. 11:12). Can you hear what Jesus is saying here? He explains in Matthew 11 that ever since He and John arrived on the scene, it has not been business as usual. Advancing the kingdom is more than just attending synagogue meetings and singing "Kumbayah" in Hebrew. No more playing patty-cake with the devil. No more letting him rule over precious souls.

This is war. And Jesus invites us to get into the action, telling us that the violent—the "forceful" ones—will lay hold of the kingdom. He is looking for us to join him in the battle of the ages, to aggressively participate in what He and John have started.

Think about it for a moment. Hold in your mind all that the Bible says about war, and battle, and being a soldier. Now consider the Christians and churches around you. Do they look like an army or a social club? There's quite a difference:

CLEARLY CONTRASTING CALLINGS

A Club Member . . .
- pursues a common interest.
- consumes some free time.
- gathers acquaintances.
- passes the time to make the day fun.
- considers preparation as optional to staying involved.
- finds courage unnecessary.

A Soldier . . .
- pursues a common mission.
- dedicates a whole life.
- gathers fellow warriors.
- seizes the day to make the battle count.
- considers preparation as crucial to staying alive.
- finds courage indispensable.

DID YOU JOIN OR ENLIST?

With the above contrasts firmly in mind, consider: When you became a Christian, did you join a club or enlist in an army? Before you answer, remember that in a club, people often have to be cajoled into staying involved ("Please help us with the fundraiser this

Jesus didn't give His life to start a social club; His church was meant to be an army.

month"). Or they have to be begged to come back ("We'll try to keep you happy and entertained—really!"). But in an army, the commander's attitude is, "Please don't come back unless you are ready to give your all." (Jesus put it like this: "Anyone else want to leave?").

My point: Jesus didn't give His life to start a social club; His church was meant to be an army. If this is the case, then we are to be soldiers, enlisted men and women. And certain key qualities of a good soldier will apply to our service in the Kingdom.

A good soldier keeps his eye on the battlefield. As I've said, most Christians don't realize there's a real war going on. They view our struggle as purely symbolic. That attitude reminds me of the war games so popular in executive training programs. High-powered execs can pay to drive tanks and compete against other members of their team as they attempt to avoid fake land mines and locate assigned coordinates. There are no bullets, of course, other than the occasional splash of wash-off paint. It is a make-believe war in which one team always gets to win.

Not so in our real combat! There is nothing symbolic about 33 million teens under withering fire. Nor is it symbolic for the teens caught in the vortex of MTV's hypnotic spell as it attempts to transform them into mooks and midriffs. You haven't heard these terms? Charles Colson explains:

The mook is a character created to appeal to adolescent males, characterized by "infantile, boorish behavior" and trapped in a state of "perpetual adolescence." Mooks are a staple on MTV.

The midriff is . . . a "highly sexualized, world-weary sophisticate" who manages to retain a bit of the little girl. Shows like Boston Public and singers like Britney Spears provide America's midriffs-in-training with role models to emulate.

Even more menacing are the McMorals taught by electronic game companies. Colonel Dave Grossman, a former Army Ranger who researched the psychology of killing in combat, says violent video and computer games are conditioning teenagers to be violent. And then along comes Hollywood, telling kids through movies like Teaching Mrs. Tingle, Urban Legend, and Scream II that violence and killing are cool. Should anyone be surprised when kids act on these messages?[1]

Mooks, midriffs, and McMorals abound in our dysfunctional families. That's why this isn't a pretend war for the millions of teens whose parents divorce each year (many of whom claim to be Christians). It's also why, each week in my travels, I see thousands stream forward asking God to help them forgive their parents for the tragic brokenness in which they've been raised. The pain is real, and these kids are the casualties of war. Their wounds range from the secrecy of emotional abuse, to the desperate loneliness of Internet addiction, to the misery of living under the same roof with parents who are strangers to them.

the pain is real, and these kids are the casualties of war.

Many are just so absorbed in today's destructive media entertainment business that they don't realize the damage being done, and neither do their parents. Others, like 13-year-old Beth, are hurting so much inside they decide to start cutting their bodies to distract themselves from the inner pain. She wrote me recently describing how she started:

Dear Ron,

i'm in a really bad place right now. i'm just craving something, anything ... i don't know what. i don't know what to do. i want my box cutter. i want to take a bunch of random pills again. i want to starve myself to death ... idk.

i haven't cut too bad for a while. i'm still eating, altho i hate myself for it. i haven't taken pills since the first/last time i did it a month ago.

i just hate me ... or maybe not. i just don't care about anything at all. it was so much easier not to care ... but now i can't make myself care anymore ... i don't know what to do. God feels sooo far away ... i stopped even praying for a long time.

She then wrote this articulate poem:

I'm Fine

I bleed away my problems
I scratch them all away
My problems drip away from me
And slither down the drain
My problems are dissolved in crimson
My scarlet poison makes them die
A piece of metal shatters them
And through my veins the pieces fly
These scars upon my skin
Tell tales of secret pain

But come and listen to them
Of the truth I'm not ashamed
My problems are hidden from you
I hide them oh so well
What's wrong? I tell you nothing
'Cause you can't save me from this hell

For Beth, this is a real war. She is shedding real blood.

A good soldier keeps his focus on what is happening at the battlefield's front lines. Have you ever seen an interview with one of the wounded in a military hospital? Time after time these heroic young people say, "I just want to get back to my unit, back with my brothers who are still out there." No matter how bad the injuries, their eyes stay fixed on the front lines. These are true soldiers.

WARTIME VS PEACETIME MENTALITY

After the terrorist attacks on September 11, 2001, we Americans suddenly realized there is an enemy and that we must fight him. The president said, "We are now at war." But a wartime mentality is completely different from a peacetime mentality.

Peacetime Mentality
- Maintaining a self-improvement orientation: We seek the latest luxuries and newest toys that will produce status.
- Focusing on personal economy: wages, promotions, career-planning—geared for advancement.

Wartime Mentality
- Maintaining a survival orientation: We seek the absolute necessities and effective weapons that will produce victory.
- Focusing on national economy: labor, production, and leadership—geared for winning.

continued

▪ Centering free time on recreational pursuits: supporting our entertainment needs.	▪ Giving free time to volunteer efforts: supporting our troops' needs.
▪ Complaining about the trivial: issues regarding routine inconveniences and discomfort.	▪ Enduring the "hardship as a soldier" (2 Tim. 2:3): issues regarding life-threatening trials and persecution.
▪ Imagining theoretical enemies.	▪ Facing real enemies.

Which mentality most often characterizes your outlook?

A good soldier lives the code. Joining any branch of the military means taking on certain inherent obligations. Soldiers know that upon enlisting their lifestyles will change dramatically. They know the "code" before signing up, so it isn't a surprise when their commanding officer insists they arise at 4 A.M., exercise, do drills, and get to work. It's all part of the package. They have no say over their way of life any more; they knew that going into the deal.

It is not an option to say to the commander, "Well, I really don't feel like doing push-ups right now." Even the thought is absurd.

Joining God's army also includes an inherent lifestyle that our loving Commander-in-Chief insists we live. When we become Christians we declare our loyalty to the person of Christ and to the lifestyle He requires of us. Romans 6:17 states it plainly: "You wholeheartedly obeyed the form of teaching to which you were entrusted." Some who come to Christ are very committed to Him—"personally"—but their way of life shows they haven't embraced the teaching and have not enlisted as soldiers. Others are so into the rules or regulations that they have never really embraced Christ and His pure grace; therefore, they become entangled in the works of righteousness symptomatic of empty religion. Either of these extremes can keep us from a passionate relationship with Christ fueled by a grateful commitment to follow His code of life as a soldier would.

As enlisted soldiers, we can't silently vote on which part of the Bible we feel like living from day to day. As if God's code (His Word) is up for debate! Yet we say apparently spiritual things like, "I just don't feel led," in order to validate our . . . disobedience.

As soldiers, we go to church services every Sunday because we want to learn how God wants us to live. He is looking for the kind of commitment that says, "Even if I don't understand why You want me to do it, I will obey." But we tend to think, "If I only knew why, then I would do it." We think that somehow God is plotting to keep us from fun. Strangely, we become wary of the greatest Lover of our souls.

When my children were small, I would grab their hands and say a firm "No" if one of them were reaching out to put a finger into an electrical socket. If she reached again, I would swat her hand and say "No" even more firmly. If she persisted, I would pull her away and swat her bottom with a "No, no!" In the mind of a toddler, this could seem mean. In fact, however, I was doing what any loving parent would do to protect a child from injury. Similarly, we can trust our loving Father. We can obey Him and His code of life laid out in His Word—even if we don't understand why He commands us with firm "No's" (and lots of "Yes's").

A good soldier finds his assignment. I've never met anyone who enlisted in the army just so he could go through boot camp.

as enlisted soldiers,
we can't silently vote
on which part of the Bible
we feel like living from day to day.

there is an assignment that only you can fill. people are waiting to be rescued until you find that assignment.

Instead, enlistees know that boot camp is just preparatory; it's not the final goal. After this intense period of training, they anticipate being assigned to a mission that will make a difference in the world. There's a place for them to plug into, and in doing so they will advance the cause of the army. They didn't join in order to sit on the sidelines and watch the action from afar. They never intended to sit around and listen to generals tell stories about strategy and tactics. No, they want to make those stories.

Too often Christians have been curious about the war, hoping to see the highlights from it, but unaware that they have a battle mission. This is evidence they have not truly enlisted. Every enlisted soldier knows he or she has a place to fill. Club members find jobs, hobbies, activities, and stuff to fill their time, but a soldier is fully engaged in his assignment.

There is an assignment that only you can fill. People are waiting to be rescued until you find that assignment. Yet how many church goers assume they've met their obligations to the Commander simply by showing up at services and dropping something in the offering plate? They watch in amazement when a few daring peers venture out to share their faith or travel to the mission field. They don't think or live like a soldier. Have they ever even enlisted?

It's as if we're sitting at a ball game to root for our favorite team. We cheer for the pastor when he wins a new convert. We celebrate when the missionary tells of the souls she's reached. We even congratulate a new believer when he comes to church for the first time. This is all normal behavior for someone who isn't on the team, someone in the stands observing. But when you get on the team, watching just won't be good enough. You want to play.

The soldier cries out to know his assignment. The team member says, "Put me in, Coach; I want to play!" And Christians who've enlisted for spiritual battle in a real war for real lives come before God with humble hearts pleading, "O Lord, show me my part. I want to be deployed into the battle for this generation! Please show me my mission."

WILL YOU SURRENDER THE CIVILIAN LIFE?

Army recruiters run offices all over America, trolling for high school graduates. They get no points if young people just visit the office and talk about enlisting. Too many Christians go to the "recruiter" on Sunday and sing about the army. They go back on Wednesday and pray about joining. They may even have tears running down their faces as they reveal their desire to be a part of God's great cause. They come back again and again to the recruiter's office. But they never enlist.

When you enlist, you belong to them. You no longer have the say-so over your life, because others now own you, 24-7. And they have

I NEED HELP please where do i start?
Well, i'm 17 and will be 18 soon. when i wuz 15 i gave my so-called life to god. At least i thought i did. after i gave my life to god I started doin things i never did before. i got into smokin, drinkin. Can't stop, i try to but i just cant. i dont know i got pain inside and im lettin it all grow inside. i dont know how to deal with it i been slittin my arms now tho not to bad. can you please help please. — *"Shorty"*

you've given up the right to do what you want. you are in full submission to Someone else.

all your activities planned for you. After enlisting, you can't say: "Hey, I'm going out to sit by the pool for a while." You've given up the right to do what you want. You are in full submission to Someone else.

Have you enlisted?

West Point is the United States Army's premier leadership training school. For two hundred years this institution has been refining our military leadership to ensure that the U.S.A. has the finest army in the world. Visiting there, I wanted to observe the ceremony experienced by the freshmen "plebes" on their very first day. The families all gather on a grandstand with their soon-to-be freshmen. Before them lies a vast, meticulously manicured lawn leading to a huge stone edifice with massive arches: West Point.

After the commanders tell the plebes that they are "the nation's best," the plebes stand, walk down the steps onto the lawn, and move toward the arches. Their parents watch silently as their babies walk away from them . . . until they finally disappear behind those stone walls. This is the last time they will ever see these young people as civilians. If the parents stay for the day and see the students later, they'll encounter a complete transformation—of hair, of clothes, of demeanor. West Point makes a dramatic statement about enlistment: it means walking away from civilian existence.

Too many of us have never walked away from civilian life. We've never walked away from the world and enlisted. This is strange, because Jesus clearly said to His disciples: "If anyone would come after me, he must deny himself and take up his cross and follow me. For whoever wants to save his life will lose it, but whoever loses his life for me will find it" (Matt. 16:24-25). This is His invitation to enlist, His call to deny ourselves, His challenge to give ourselves away and find our assignment in His Kingdom.

The apostle Paul said it too: "I have been crucified with Christ and I no longer live, but Christ lives in me" (Gal. 2:20). He also says that we've been "bought at a price" (1 Cor. 7:23). As soldiers we are no longer the owners of our lives. Our joy as a soldier is to find our Commander's assignment and throw our lives into embracing Him and His mission for us.

And please realize that enlisting in God's army is a deep work in our hearts, a work of ultimate surrender. Here's what I mean: One busy day I was called upon by the parents of a 17-year-old girl named Diana. They said they were visiting from out of town and told me that Diana had been raised in church and was a good Christian. She had just returned from a mission trip with Teen Mania's Global Expeditions that summer, and this was to be the subject of our conversation. It seems that as soon as Diana got off the plane, she called home. But instead of saying "Hi, I missed you," or telling her parents about the trip, she immediately demanded writing utensils:

"Mom, get a piece of paper and a pen!"
"Hi, honey, how you are?"
"Get a pen and paper right away!"
"Why? What's the matter?"
"Please just get a paper and pen right way!"

After Mom returned to the phone with the utensils, Diana said, "Write down this date." The date she mentioned had occurred during the mission trip.

"What is so important about this date, Diana?"

Diana replied with a statement her parents had never heard before. Her mother looked at me with tears streaming down her

an enlisted soldier is not doing his commander a favor by tending to his assignment. he is doing his duty.

cheeks as she told me Diana's words: "Mom, that was the day that I died."

Mom then told me that her little girl has never been the same. Since returning home she has lived to serve, constantly reaching out to others in her school. She now exists to give her life away to reach others. She died to her selfish desires. She enlisted.

An enlisted soldier is not doing his commander a favor by tending to his assignment. He is doing his duty. He is doing what he signed up to do. If we are to rescue this generation, we must enlist. Our commitment can't be just a phase or an "emphasis" for a month. We won't be doing this as a favor to a church leader or to get a parent or youth pastor off our back. No, it is the moral obligation of every soldier to engage in the battle until the battle is won.

It is time to enlist. Will you join me in this prayer as we stand at the brink of battle together?

My Father,

I ask You to forgive me for mere club membership in Your family. I am desperately sorry for enjoying the goodness of Your forgiveness and passively looking on while others fight for souls. I ask You to take ownership of my will. I submit all my rights to You. I deny myself, refusing to live merely for my own good. I will keep my eyes on the battle, submitting to Your code even when I don't understand, and engaging wholeheartedly in my assignment. I transfer the ownership of all that I am into Your hands. I no longer claim say-so for my life but gladly live according to Your mandate. In response to Your love for me, I will live outside my comfort zone in the battle zone to rescue a hurting world.

In Jesus' name I pray. Amen.

---

[1] Charles Colson, "Merchants of Cool," in Christianity Today, June 11, 2001, Vol. 45, No. 8, p. 112.

understanding the crisis

For the past three decades, many dedicated youth ministries, volunteer groups, and organizations have passionately reached out to young people across America. For all the good mentoring work they've done, it has not been enough. They have failed to keep pace with the destructive forces attacking our youth.

Segments of the media, pop culture, and the business world have been working harder and with better resources to capture a generation by restructuring its values, especially in the area of sexuality. For a few minutes, we want you to peer into a teen's world and see what they see.

In this part of the book, you'll take a close look at the methods of cultural sexualization, how it denigrates our children's morals, and how we can begin to respond. One thing is certain: we can no longer afford to remain silent and do nothing.

CHAPTER FOUR

Secondhand Sex

Only a few short years ago, you could walk into most any public place and have a good coughing fit. Cigarette smoke wafted from wall to wall in restaurants, office buildings, and hotel lobbies. If you weren't a smoker, you at least felt like one.

But then came the protests. Smokers were accused of violating fellow citizens' rights to breathe! Many fresh-air seekers complained but were, at first, perceived as a trouble-making minority trying to trample others' rights. The grumbling grew louder, though, until scientists began studying the actual effects of "secondhand smoke." Once the harmful consequences became known, non-smokers had the ammunition they needed to battle for real change.

Laws were passed to forbid smoking in many public buildings. And huge, class-action lawsuits forced the producers of tobacco

you never intended any of this.
nevertheless, this generation
has been "educated" before
being ready.

pollution to pay for the harm they'd done over the years. The point: No one should be allowed to profit while harming other people.

But what of our cultural environment these days? With the constant push to "take God out of the public eye," we have lost the visible reminders of our Christian heritage. And, ever so gradually, we have allowed more perversity in the public forum. To put it bluntly, our *secularization has led to sexualization.*

You don't need to see any data to know that our society is now saturated with sex. Think about how many times you've stood at a checkout counter and told your kids, "Don't look at that." How many times you've watched television together and had to say, "Look away, please." How many times you've fielded questions from a pre-teen— about sexual things you never knew until well into married life. Even the public billboards have become pollution to our souls as nearly naked women proclaim, "We dare to bare all," and so-called gentlemen's clubs proudly advertise as if they were upstanding members of the local business community.

Each instance robs our children of innocence. It also robs the parents of their right to protect young minds and hearts. You never intended for them to see what flashed before them as you were flipping through public airwave channels. You never intended any of this. Nevertheless, this generation has been "educated" before being ready and without proper moral explanations of God's design for sex in marriage. We, as parents, can only pick up the leftovers and do our best to help our children live moral lives.

This might be a winnable battle for you and your children—if you were always with them, 24 hours a day. But that's hardly realistic. So they are overwhelmed by the sexual, just as we are. Like second-hand smoke, it invades our public places and our private spaces, it permeates the nooks and crannies of our lives, sneaks through the cracks under the door, and silently wafts through the atmosphere of our family lives, subverting every attempt at moral teaching and responsible living. It's called secondhand sex.

THE SCOURGE OF SECONDHAND SEX

It is everywhere, and our children are breathing it in. There are virtually no safe zones, no protected public airwaves, no magazine racks that aren't blaring some kind of "best sex tips" headline.

Even PG-rated movies contain references and innuendos that demand explanation to a curious mind. Teen magazines, especially for girls, abound with advice on how to French kiss and "how you'll know it's time to have intercourse." (In fact, they don't even give it the dignity of calling it "sexual intercourse" anymore; it's known as "hooking up.") Many teens, after learning about these things in

it invades our public places and our private spaces, it permeates the nooks and crannies of our lives, sneaks through the cracks under the door, and silently wafts through the atmosphere of our family lives. it's called secondhand sex.

supposedly respected youth mags, are hooking up with friends, even in the absence of any romantic involvement.

Is the pollution bothering anyone else?

And don't assume this is all just the uninformed ranting of a nit-picking super-moralist. You see, as with the history of secondhand smoke, the scientists have finally showed up to study secondhand sex. A new study conducted by the Medical Institute for Sexual Health (funded by the Centers for Disease Control) indicates the obvious: Teens are bombarded with sexual images from pop media. "All we really know is that kids are overexposed to sex," says Dr. Joe McIlhaney, Jr., president of the Institute. "It's everywhere ... [so] even if they tried, kids can't escape it."

The research revealed that the average teen spends three to four hours in front of the tube daily and that an average of 6.7 scenes in every hour of programming includes sexual topics. Researchers concluded that teens constantly exposed to such sexual depictions are "more likely than other adolescents" to have more permissive attitudes toward premarital sex and "to think that having sex is bene-ficial." Likewise, teens listen to nearly 40 hours of radio a week. More than 25 percent of teen-targeted radio segments contain sexual content; 42 percent of top-selling CDs contain sexual content that is "pretty explicit" or "very explicit." Nine to 17 year olds use the Internet four days per week (two hours at a time). Of those who use computers, 61 percent go online, 14 percent of who say they see things they "wouldn't want their parents to know about."[1]

Consider the huge ramifications of the report we mentioned in Chapter 3. Remember that the study of 1,792 teens, ages 12 to 17, showed that watching sex on TV influences teens to have sex. It doesn't take a genius to figure this out, but now the facts are in. A 2004 study by the RAND Corporation (funded by the U.S. National Institute of Child Health), published in Pediatrics, shows the clear connection:

Teens who watch a lot of such sexualized programming are twice as likely to engage in sexual intercourse themselves....Rebecca Collins, a RAND Corporation psychologist who led the study, said, "This is the strongest evidence yet that the sexual content of television programs encourages adolescents to initiate sexual intercourse and other sexual activities. The impact of television viewing is so large that even a moderate shift in the sexual content of adolescent TV watching could have a substantial effect on their sexual behavior."[2]

Clearly, the teenage brain is unable to "make sense" of all the pornographic stimuli it receives or to protect itself against it. Programs involving explicit sex talk had the same effect as programs where the sex was seen, causing even 12-year-old children to think pornographic behavior was normal, propelling many into copycat sexual actions and causing nightmares and other direct signs of anxiety.[3] Other findings about our youth, gathered by the Alan Guttmacher Institute, include these eye-opening statistics:

SEXUAL EXPOSURE OF TEENS

- Average age of first sex: 15.8 years
- Average length of first sexual relationship: 3.8 months
- 24.3% of adolescents reported having first sex during the same month as the start of the relationship (37.5% had sex 1 to 3 months after the start of the relationship and 40.1% after 4 months)
- 23.4% of first sexual relationships were "one-night stands" (21.2% for girls and 26.5% for guys)
- Girls reported their first sexual partner was 1.8 years older, on average; guys said 0.1 years younger
- 16.7% of adolescents (20.6% girls and 11.2% boys) who took virginity pledges became sexually active[4]

LATELY I HAVE

been talking to this guy i have known
for a long time. Just recently he got
really bad doing drugs and having sex
and getting drunk and stuff and he is
sixteen ... i know what he is doing is bad
and honestly i like him a little and he likes me
and is trying to get me to have sex with him. i already
kissed him and i KNOW what i did is wrong and that he is a bad
guy and that i need to get away from him but he is everywhere i
go! even church and my house in the summertime! What can i
do to get away from him? —*Rachel*

It's interesting to note that 67 percent of sexually experienced
teens (77 percent of girls and 60 percent of boys) wish they had
waited longer to become sexually active. But how many teens said it
was embarrassing to admit they were virgins? Twenty-six percent.

Students do overestimate their peers' sexual experiences,
however. In grades nine through twelve, 68 percent of students said
their peers have had sex. According to the 2001 Youth Risk Behavior
Survey conducted by the Center for Disease Control, only 46 percent
of teens in those grades have had sex.[5]

Yet while the teen intercourse rate has declined from 54 percent
in 1991 to 47 percent in 2003, odds are it's merely because teens have
replaced intercourse with oral sex.[6] And recent studies show it's not
uncommon for high-school students to have sex with someone
they're not dating. A 2001 survey conducted by Bowling Green State
University in Ohio found that of the 55 percent of local eleventh
graders who engaged in intercourse, 60 percent said they'd had sex
with a partner who was no more than a friend. That number would
most likely be higher if the study would have asked about oral sex.[7]

Such attitudes came from somewhere. Our moldable teens are fashioned by media peddlers doing whatever they need to do to get the attention of a new generation of buyers. They sell a lot, make a lot, and thrust an unknowingly manipulated generation into social chaos. One expert commented: "Teens are unwittingly swept up in the social mores of the moment, and it's certainly not some alternative they're choosing to keep from getting hurt emotionally. The fact is, girls don't enjoy hookups nearly as much as boys, no matter what they say at the time. They're only doing it because that's what the boys want."[8] We can hear the heart cries of teens of both genders caught up in this battle—

- "I know the Bible says you can't have sex before marriage. But why can't you, if you're in love with the person? It doesn't feel wrong."—Kendra, 14

- "My boyfriend and I don't want to mess around anymore. But how do we keep this commitment? I never realized how powerful passion can be."—Shari, 15

- "Kids at school are pressuring me and my girlfriend to have sex. I want to wait until marriage, but I worry about how this makes me look."—Darryl, 17

- "I feel cut off from God. I want to do what's right, but I can't seem to. Recently I had sex with a guy, thinking that it would bring us closer. I know now that was a mistake, and I feel totally ashamed."—Aimee, 16

These young people have learned too much, too early by their exposure to secondhand sex. Their minds have been violated, and they have lost the innocence and purity the Creator intended for their sexual relationship in marriage.

science now has proven the connection between this saturation-exposure and the sexual behavior of our children.

As we've seen, science now has proven the connection between this saturation-exposure and the sexual behavior of our children. It is a devastating, destructive connection: Teens have lost their virginity, they have lost their physical health, they have lost their moral compass. Many have also lost their dreams for the future by getting pregnant out of wedlock—and a lot of them have lost their babies in this process. Some have even lost their lives.

All the while, the producers of this sex pollution are making more money. Does something about this seem terribly wrong? But it gets worse. I'm afraid we'll have to enter the sleazy world of pornography to know the true horror.

POINT-AND-CLICK TO PORN

The first generation of point-and-click Internet porn can now directly demonstrate to us the damage done to soul and psyche. There was a day when it would be embarrassing to walk up to a checkout counter and ask for a porn magazine. And few respectable citizens would risk being seen entering an adult video store. It was quite difficult to feed one's lust anonymously in the days before the World Wide Web.

Those days are over. A limitless variety of porn lingers just a click away, ready to be delivered via high-speed cyber connections straight to the anonymous comfort of your computer chair. Gone is the shame of having to ask for "one of those"—quick, in a bag, please!—from the nice lady at the cash register.

This great new technology we all benefit from is also wreaking havoc on our kids. Point and click to whatever you want—or don't want. The odds of avoiding it seem hardly fair, because kids don't even have to deliberately go looking for the garbage: By 1999 "one in five children between the ages of 10 and 17 received a sexual solicitation over the Internet, and one in 33" were approached for a direct contact in some manner.[9]

Based on her Department of Justice study, Judith Reisman, president of the California Protective Parents Association, states that "much of the multi-billion dollar pornography industry focused on attracting 12- to 17-year-old boys to ensure lifetime addict-consumers."[10] This juvenile marketing strategy is arguably similar to that employed by Big Tobacco, but the target market seems even younger. The average age of first Internet exposure to pornography is 11 years old.[11]

Let that sink in. Our young ones are being addicted at an alarming rate. They get a taste of lewd material from the store, and then from a commercial. They read more about it in a fashion magazine. They hear constant references to it in "family hour" sitcoms. They are bombarded with it by MTV and all the music videos and other shows that provoke them to want to live like, apparently, "everybody else" is living.

SINCE I CAN remember i have struggled with homosexuality, at least twelve years. For the past two years i have been looking up sites on the Internet and chatting online with some homosexuals doing some questionable things. Today I experimented with using the phone also. I am a virgin since that i have never had sexual relations with another person, however i have struggled with masturbation. I am asking for your prayers and advice. Thanks —*Nathan* "today's first base is deep kissing, now known as tonsil hockey, plus groping and fondling this and that. second base is oral sex. third base is going all the way. home plate is learning each other's names."

So when they get an e-mail that throws them to a porn site, they're already baited and ready to become addicted. That's why Family Safe Media can report that 80 percent of 15 to 17 year olds have had multiple hard-core porn exposures. And 90 percent of 8 to 16 year olds have viewed porn online (most while doing homework).[12]

It's shocking, but we need to know what's really going on. We need to understand what is provoking so much of this activity among teens. Consider these four trends that add to the mix:

Hoping for a happy hook-up, then . . . "Bye-bye." A recent article by AFA Journal[13] reports research indicating that "hooking up" is becoming an increasingly common practice among young people today. What is hooking up in today's culture? According to the article, the College of New Jersey defines it as "petting below the waist, oral sex, or intercourse" between two people who have no intention of relating beyond a one-time physical encounter. It's hello, sex, and good-bye. The article continues:

> As reported by PluggedInOnline.com, Elizabeth Paul, psychology professor, surveyed 555 undergraduate students and found 78 percent of them had hooked up at some point, usually following the consumption of alcohol. In addition, Paul found the average number of hookups per student during their college career to be nearly 11.

Her findings parallel similar studies conducted by researchers at James Madison University and the University of Michigan, as well as claims made by author Tom Wolfe in his book *Hooking Up*. "Today's first base is deep kissing, now known as tonsil hockey, plus groping and fondling this and that. Second base is oral sex. Third base is going all the way. Home plate is learning each other's names," Wolfe writes.

Do you hear your teens talking about hooking up? It's not just innocent chatter. In fact, 36 percent of 15 to 17 year olds report that they've had oral sex.[14] However, "half of these teens do not identify oral sex as sex, according to 2003 surveys."[15]

Embracing colorful bracelets, then . . . "Snap." The latest among junior highers is horrifying: the Jelly Bracelet fad. Jelly Bracelet fashion accessories have been around since the 80s. But instead of being merely a fashion statement, they may be making a statement about your kid's sex life. These bendable pieces of colored rubber have become a sexual code to many teens. Here's a common breakdown:

Yellow: hugging
Purple: kissing
Red: lap dance
Blue: oral sex
Black: intercourse

But it's not just a testimony to past experience; it's an invitation to future hook-ups. In a game called Snap, if a boy breaks a jelly bracelet off a girl's wrist, he gets a sexual coupon for that act. Yes, many deny actually giving more than a hug or kiss if a bracelet is

we now know that pornographic visual images imprint and alter the brain, triggering an instant, involuntary, but lasting, biochemical memory trail.

snapped off of their wrist. And many will say the bracelets really are nothing more than a fashion statement. Then again, rumor also has it that participation in the game has increased due to so much publicity (many teens claim they didn't know about the game until it was publicized).

Getting a brain makeover, then . . . "Poisoned!" Since the 1970s the brains of almost all youths have been restructured by what is known as pornography's "erototoxins," a big word for a type of brain poisoning. In a 1979 survey of over six hundred boys and girls aged 15 to 18, Aaron Hass found that almost 100 percent of boys and over 90 percent of girls had "looked at sexy books or magazines . . . [and] almost 60 percent of boys and over 40 percent of girls had seen a sexual movie." Hass concluded that most of the children believed the pornographic "information" they saw and many engaged in copycat sex acts. Almost all teenagers have seen or read some form of pornography. "Pornography provides teenagers with a sexual education," Hass reported.[16]

And the brain is educated toward addiction. In a hearing before the U.S. Senate Committee, Dr. Judith Reisman quoted neurologist Richard Restak:

> Thanks to the latest advances in neuroscience, we now know that pornographic visual images imprint and alter the brain, triggering an instant, involuntary, but lasting, biochemical memory trail, arguably subverting the First Amendment

by overriding the cognitive speech process. This is true of so-called "soft-core" and "hard-core" pornography. And once new neuro-chemical pathways are established they are difficult or impossible to delete.

Pornographic images also cause secretion of the body's "fight or flight" sex hormones. This triggers excitatory transmitters and produces non-rational, involuntary reactions; intense arousal states that overlap sexual lust—now with fear, shame, and/or hostility and violence. Media erotic fantasies become deeply imbedded, commonly coarsening, confusing, motivating, and addicting many of those exposed. Pornography triggers myriad kinds of internal, natural drugs that mimic the "high" from a street drug. Addiction to pornography is addiction to what I dub erototoxins— mind-altering drugs produced by the viewer's own brain.

How does this "brain sabotage" occur? Brain scientists tell us that "in 3/10 of a second a visual image passes from the eye through the brain, and whether or not one wants to, the brain is structurally changed and memories are created. We literally 'grow new brain' with each visual experience."[17]

Grooming by addictive viewing, then . . . "Jail time?"
Reports of suspected child pornography climbed 39 percent in 2004, according to the National Center for Missing and Exploited Children, which also just released the following report from New Zealand on teenage users as sex offenders:

> Teenagers are the biggest viewers of child pornography, with a study warning … [that] the youngest offender was 14. Young people aged 15 to 20 were the single biggest demographic group, accounting for one-quarter of all child porn users tracked and caught by investigators …

Customs last year saw a "massive growth" in the number and seriousness of horrific child porn intercepted by officials . . . An "association" between viewing child porn and offending against children [is implicated] . . . Some teens viewing and trading child porn had been lured via the Internet by adults "grooming them" with the material.[18]

One law enforcement spokesperson (Liz Butterfield, quoted in the article above) said, "It's essential that sex offender treatment is provided for all ages, but especially for the younger ones." However, a U.S. Government Accounting Office study identified no success rate for sex offender "treatment."[19] Why? Because, according to Dr. Mary Anne Layden, "images dominate rational thought, especially in the teenage developing brain."[20] Professors Satinover, Weaver, Layden and Reisman have all testified to the destructiveness of pornography's erototoxins before Senator Brownback's investigative committee on November 18, 2004. Reisman explained that the human brain obeys a "law of strength." That means "strong, fearful, arousing, and confusing sexual and sado-sexual images will always dominate, occupy, and colonize the brain and displace cognition, despite any disclaimers used in 'sex education.'"[21]

IT'S ALL ABOUT THE GATEWAY

Most of us can understand how addictions to certain physical substances get started. But how does this kind of mental addiction occur? We can liken the process to the now universally accepted principles of what are called "gateway drugs." Simply put, gateway drug use leads to hard-core drug use. It is a proven fact that most kids who use illicit drugs started out with an addiction to alcohol or tobacco. A strong link binds these two addictions.[22]

Some gateway drugs are substances that will eventually be legal to teenagers once they reach the age of 21. There are only two gateway drugs in this category: alcohol and tobacco. The Child Trends Data Bank tells us: "Use of alcohol, cigarettes, and marijuana, sometimes called gateway drugs, may increase the likelihood of other drug use. Because youth who are known to use one substance often use other substances as well, prevention programs that target multiple substances may be more successful than those that focus on only one."[23] Because of this gateway concept, the anti-drug movement strives to curb the access and usage of gateway drugs in order to keep serious addictions to a minimum.

Here's the bottom line: Isn't it overwhelmingly likely that the "soft porn" of MTV, movies, and the music industry are making it that much easier for our young ones to click into perverse, hard-core Web sites that take the corruption of their precious minds to a sickening new low?

And how big is the porn industry? It is about 57 billion dollars per year big. That is more than the combined revenue flowing into ABC, CBS, and NBC. It's more than all professional sports teams, put together, receive in a year. This industry is huge and getting bigger every day as they pull our young ones in. Look at some of the other data:

BIG BUCKS FOR PORN PEDDLERS

- $20 billion is spent worldwide on adult pornographic videos.
- $2.5 billion is spent worldwide on cable pay-per-view.
- $2.5 billion is spent worldwide on Internet pornography.
- $3 billion is generated by child pornography annually.
- 4.2 million pornographic Web sites reside on the Internet (21% of total web sites).
- 372 million pages of pornographic material fill the Internet.
- 68 million pornographic searches are requested by Internet users each day (25% of total search engine requests).
- 2.5 billion pornographic e-mails go out daily (8% of total e-mails).
- 4.5 pornographic e-mails are sent, daily, per Internet user.
- 100,000 Web sites currently offer illegal child pornography.

we were not as vigilant as we should have been, and now a moral and social catastrophe looms for our kids.

Who looks at all of this porn? Christians, you are not immune. We know that:

- *53% of Promise Keeper men viewed pornography last week.*
- *47% of Christians say pornography is a major problem in the home.*
- *Visitors to pornography sites are 72% male and 28% female[24]*

You may be thinking that, after all this bad news, what could be worse? How about this fact: The largest consumers of Internet pornography are kids in the 12 to 17 age group.[25] Therefore, can anyone deny that pornography (sexually explicit material and programming) is the most prevalent and most destructive issue facing young people today?

Where were the decent adults in America when all of this was unfolding? When the secondhand sex drifted in, we held our noses and walked away. Even as we were being wooed by all the excitement of the 21st century's new technology, we somehow missed the implications for our young ones. No reasonable adult would want their children to be exposed to the perversity described in this chapter. But it seems as though most of them are, indeed, constantly exposed. It's in the air, saturating the cultural atmosphere. We were not as vigilant as we should have been, and now a moral and social catastrophe looms for our kids. In the chapter ahead we'll look at what these trends will mean to an entire generation.

1 "Pornography Targets the Teenage Brain, Mind, Memory and Behavior: America's Children versus the Impotence Industry." Report prepared by Judith A. Reisman, Ph.D., the Institute for Media Education.

2 "Pornography Targets the Teenage Brain …," Ibid.

3 "Pornography Targets the Teenage Brain …," Ibid.

4 Alan Guttmacher Institute, "Patterns of Contraception Use Within Teenagers' First Sexual Relationships," CPYU's Youth Culture e-Update #51, 1/14/04.

5 National Campaign to Prevent Teen Pregnancy (True Lies E-mail Update, Jan. 2004).

6 "Friends, Friends with Benefits, and the Benefits of the Local Mall," *New York Times*, 5/30/04.

7 "Friends, Friends with Benefits …," Ibid.

8 "Friends, Friends with Benefits …," Ibid.

9 J. Mitchell Kimberly, et. al., The exposure of youth to unwanted sexual material on the Internet. *Youth & Society*, Vol. 34 no. 3, March 2003, pp. 330-358.

10 Judith Reisman, *Soft Porn Plays Hard Ball: Its Tragic Effects on Women, Children and the Family* (Lafayette, LA: Huntington House, 1991.

11 "Pornography Statistics 2003," Family Safe Media.

12 "Pornography Statistics 2003," Ibid.

13 "More Teens 'Hook Up,'" by AFA Journal (Agape Press), January 14, 2005.

14 As reported by the Center for Parent/Youth Understanding, quoted in the article by AFA Journal, January 14, 2005.

15 Surveys conducted by the Kaiser Family Foundation and *Seventeen* magazine, reported in the article by AFA Journal, January 14, 2005.

16 Aaron Hass, *Teenage Sexuality* (New York: Macmillan, 1979).

17 Speech by Judith Reisman given at a Science, Technology, and Space Hearing: "The Science Behind Pornography Addiction," Thursday, November 18, 2004. Available on the Web at: **http://commerce.senate.gov/hearings/testimony.cfm?id=1343&wit_id=3910**.

18 *New Zealand Herald*, January 15, 2005. On the Web at: **http://www.nzherald.co.nz/index.cfm?c_id=5&ObjectID=10006544**.

19 See **drjudithreisman.org**, White papers on the FBI and DOJ reduction of child sexual abuse reports for the GOA study on sex-offender treatment failure studies.

20 Testimony for U.S. Senate Committee on Commerce, Science, and Transportation, November 18, 2004, by Mary Anne Layden, Ph.D., Co-Director Sexual Trauma and Psychopathology Program. She is also direct of the Education Center for Cognitive Therapy, the Department of Psychiatry, at the University of Pennsylvania.

21 Reisman, "The Science Behind Pornography Addiction," Op. Cit.

22 "Gateway Drugs," by A. J. Czerwinskia. Available on the Web at **http://www.goerie.com/niegatewaytab/gateway_drugs.html**.

23 Child Trends Data Bank, "Substance Free Youth," 6/8/04.

24 "Pornography Statistics 2003," Family Safe Media.

25 Ibid.

CHAPTER FIVE

denigration of a generation

Rod   Blagojevich   wants   to   save   American youth.[1] This Democrat governor of Illinois firmly believes his success will depend upon stopping retailers from hawking M-rated video games to kids under 17. He has his reasons. Chief among them: the storylines of games like JFK Reloaded, in which players compete for the chance to assassinate the former president.

Outraged, Blagojevich is proposing bills to slap a $5,000 fine— or a year in jail—upon anyone who tries to rent or sell inappropriate video content to underage youngsters. He contends the $7 billion industry is actually targeting the younger kids. Therefore, "just as a child buying cigarettes is inappropriate, just as a child buying alcohol is inappropriate, just as a child buying pornography is inappropriate, the same kind of thinking applies to violent video games and graphic sexual video games."

Perhaps the good governor is aware of Michigan State University's recent survey findings: Eighth-grade boys play violent video games for about 23 hours a week, and girls for 12 hours a week. Also lending support to his cause is a 2003 study by the FTC reporting that 69 percent of 13 to 16 year olds who tried to purchase M-rated games . . . were able to do so.

Mr. Blagojevich will easily succeed, right?

Wrong. In spite of all the alarming call-to-action statistics, *Time* magazine reports: "Blagojevich is in for a tough fight."

DRAMATIC CHANGE, DEADLY CORRUPTION

Here's the big question. Why would Blagojevich be in for a tough fight? How could that be possible—assuming all adults surely want every young person to grow up with a healthy, peace-loving character?

But we've come a long way, haven't we? During the past 50 years of our nation's history, social norms have become more "enlightened." These days, we can hardly imagine the uproar from viewers when "I Love Lucy" showed Ricky and Lucy sleeping in the bedroom together—in separate beds. Today nudity and perversity pour forth from the typical family television network.

We all know things have slid downhill, but just how far have they gone? When teachers in 1940 were asked to identify top problems in the public schools, they said, "talking out of turn, chewing gum, making noise." In 1990, teachers said, "drug and alcohol abuse, pregnancy, suicide, rape, robbery, and assault."[2] These are major, costly behavior changes reflecting a transformation of the minds and memories of the average child.

How did it happen? How did we get to the point of fighting a government leader who simply wants to keep teenagers from gorging themselves on hour upon hour of bloody, sexualized spectacle?

Certain societal trends have gradually produced this generation-corrupting situation. Let's look closer at what's been happening since the 1960s.

A business-dominated culture takes over. Numerous and simultaneous changes suggest that our world may, in fact, be catapulting toward a new era, undergoing a massive and foundational shift. Consider:

SEISMIC CULTURAL SHIFTS

- From the time of Adam until the Israelites crossed over into the Promised Land, families and tribes ruled the world.
- From the time of Joshua until the crucifixion of Christ, armies ruled the world.
- From the time of Rome until the Age of Enlightenment, religion ruled the world.
- From the Age of Enlightenment until the fall of Communism, politics ruled the world.
- From the fall of the Berlin Wall for as far as the mind can imagine, business will rule the world.

Isn't it obvious that business dominates society today? And a particularly subversive mantra prevails: *"If I have the ability to make money at something, then I have the right to do it."* If I can, then I ought.

The beauty of this ethical code is its pristine simplicity. The ugly flipside is that it allows for no objective moral compass to guide our business institutions, and our young ones suffer. You see, there's a big difference between having the means and having the moral mandate.

We have, apparently, ignored that crucial distinction. Thus our notion of free enterprise dominates in a world of no standards. Any

there's a big difference between having the means and having the moral mandate.

product, if it makes money, is a good product. So the Golden Rule has been redefined: "The one with the gold ... rules." If you're able to make money at something, and you gather enough money to pay either lobbyists or attorneys to keep you out of court, then it's okay to continue.

The approach works. Violent video games, for example, sell quite well. But as a result, our young ones have been softened to the idea of beating and killing another human being. So we have the recent story from Houston of an 11 year old killing his father, shooting him through the back seat of the family car. And because there are no parameters regarding what is acceptable sexual content in our media, we hear of another 11-year-old boy molesting an 87-year-old woman. Extreme cases, yes. But think about the overall drop in moral consciousness since the mid-20th century. Think about the lowered ethical standards, the acceptability of so much pure degradation. How could it fail to exert a powerful and damaging influence on young minds?

A morally bankrupt climate arises. The philosophy that all truth is relative has now made moral absolutes unnecessary. I won't bother to prove it with logical deductive arguments because I don't have to. Anyone with decent eyesight can see it. Let me give you just two "Scenes from a Mall," to borrow from a Woody Allen movie title:

- You walk past the Victoria's Secret and glance into the storefront window: Your eyes fall upon massive posters of half-naked women. They are "dressed" and posed in ways that thoroughly mimic what used to appear in pornographic magazines hidden behind counters in "the good old days." Now such scenes adorn life-sized displays for all to see.

- You stroll into Abercrombie & Fitch to pick up a catalog: You page through gay and lesbian depictions (set in strip clubs and shower rooms) that would have been unthinkable just a few years ago. Here's a description of one such publication:

The most overtly gay-specific that Abercrombie has ever done, these images from the Winter 2000 issue of A&F Quarterly, the company's own magalogue, depict a double wedding of the Emerson family. Ironically, the reply card responses include ..."Yes, I'd love to see two women get married." Predictably, the issue caused some controversy, something that A&F Quarterly has experienced before over depictions of nudity and the use of alcohol, due to the brand's popularity with youth ...

After generations of invisibility, in these commercials guys actually get their guys, and gals get their gals. Kisses and affectionate displays are enjoyed by same-sex couples in the imagery. Transgendered persons are a non-issue, Gay Pride is celebrated, and some commercials even seem to sell the idea of being "gay" more than the product.[3]

At the very least, such advertising teaches our young ones that to be valuable, you must flaunt your body. What kind of a toll is this taking on the self-images of our 11-, 12-, and 13-year-old daughters? What is it saying to them about how they should dress, how they should carry themselves? And what kind of a message is it sending to our pre-teen boys? How can we be comfortable with morally absent "ad men" shaping our perceptions of what a woman should be?

As our society's moral relativity is allowed to determine what young people see and hear, we end up with a self-perpetuating denigration of society. We allowed free expression to proliferate once we concluded that moral absolutes were old-fashioned. Yet, paradoxically, the politically-correct endorsers of such a philosophy hold tenaciously to their own unassailable moral absolute: It is always right to be tolerant.

A sex-saturated curriculum prevails. Formal sex education is standard practice in our public schools. Yet the major sex education accreditation agencies are economically linked to Big Pornography (see Judith Reisman's book, *Kinsey, Crimes & Consequences* for full documentation of this fact). According to Judith Reisman, most accredited school sex educators deliver sexual information and images to children that are false and often pornographic (excluding pure "abstinence educators," none of whom are officially accredited). The pornography as "education" that children are given by sex educators is especially confusing and damaging because it comes with the school system's stamp of approval. After all, sexuality experts have developed the material. What could possibly be wrong with it?

THE PRICE WE PAY

What do these societal trends end up costing us? They extract from our sons and daughters their purity, their innocence, and their perspectives on marriage and intimacy. They rob me, as a parent, of my opportunity to give my children a healthy understanding of wholesome love, romance, and intimacy. In the name of free speech and business enterprise, the impact of the forces we describe have painful ramifications for all of us.

Emotional Pain. Teenage sexual activity has generated widespread national concern. Although it has declined somewhat in recent years, the overall rate is still high. In 1997, approximately 48 percent of American teenagers of high-school age were, or had been, sexually active. One less-publicized problem with this is that, when compared to teens who are not sexually active, these kids are significantly less likely to be happy, more likely to feel depressed, and more likely to attempt suicide. Other problems associated with teen sexual activity are well-known:

- *Every day, 8,000 teenagers in the United States become infected by an STD.*
- *This year, nearly 3 million teens will become infected.*
- *About one-quarter of the nation's sexually active teens have been infected by an STD.*
- *In 2000, some 240,000 children were born to girls age 18 or younger. Nearly all these teenage mothers were unmarried.*[4]

These challenges are monumental, and we will look more closely at them below. But here, let's go to the "heart" of the problem of emotional pain surrounding teenage sexuality. It's less about lust than about ...loneliness. In a study of mid-adolescent high school students, Chap Clark wanted to go beyond the statistics to find the motivating factors behind them. He uncovered a youthful world filled

let's go to the "heart" of the
problem of emotional pain
surrounding teenage sexuality.
it's less about lust than
about . . . loneliness.

SOMETIMES I want to commit suicide. I know why, but sometimes I don't know why. I haven't told my parents yet. I tried to commit suicide about three nights ago. Actually, I don't really want to tell my parents, but I think they will find out soon. I don't know what they will say, but I do wonder about it. Please if you have any advice please please write me back. —*Holly (11)*

with longing for romance, desire for connection, and yearning for relational intimacy.

> Soon after I began this study . . . I thought that high school boys and girls would easily and constantly be swept up in a world of sexual lust and wild, irresponsible elational dalliances. I was surprised to realize that for most mid-adolescents the issue of sex has lost its mystique and has become almost commonplace. They have been conditioned to expect so much from sex and have been so tainted by overexposure and the emptiness of valueless sexual banter and play that they have become laissez-faire in their attitudes and even jaded. As one student told me, "Sex is a game and a toy, nothing more." As I was to find out, it is also more than that—it is a temporary salve for the pain and loneliness resulting from abandonment.[5]

Do you feel compassion welling up in your heart for young people today? God has built into all of us an intense longing for closeness and wholeness. If the fulfillment of this longing can only be found in Him, the Infinite Lord, then those who aren't clinging to Him daily will attach their longing to false infinites, other objects of affection. It is a temptation for all of us. As writer Ronald Rolheiser put it: "Our spirituality is, ultimately, about what we do with our desire."[6]

"It appears that today's mid-adolescents are crying out for attention and affection," says Chap Clark. What will we do as we observe their pain? Yes, our battle concerns a behavioral phenomenon, well-documented statistically. But at its heart is a passionate spiritual and emotional craving. How will we respond?

Addictive Rewiring. Another price we pay for our sex-saturation is the plague of addiction. As we saw in the previous chapter, pornographic erototoxins always bypass cognition and speech, reaching the right brain instantly to trigger excitatory transmitters and to overcome inhibitory transmitter functions. The human brain is restructured, altered, and permanently changed by each pornographic image. Once glimpsed on a billboard, television, computer screen, or magazine cover—whether or not one wants—erototoxic images invade and occupy the human brain, mind, and memory. The chart below recaps the established facts and processes we've detailed.

BASIC PSYCHOPHARMACOLOGICAL DATA

- Pornographic images are neurochemically processed as real in the teenage brain.[7] Penetrating as "excitatory transmissions... in less than 1/1000 of a second,"[8] pornography's erototoxins shape the teenage brain on all three brain levels—
  Stage 1: The teenage brain is "alert and aware" of pornography as "reality."
  Stage 2: The teenage brain "stores" pornography as "environmental information."
  Stage 3: By "monitoring and correcting" teenage conduct, pornography injures the teenage users' health and well-being.

continued

- Erototoxic fantasies invade and commonly overcome reality. Males (and more and more females) unconsciously seek to bond with the women they autoerotically bonded with as juveniles on magazine pages or on computer screens.[9]

In light of the addictive rewiring of the brain, we could say that choice is denied the victim. This lack of choice in the human brain largely explains why the National Center for Missing and Exploited Children "logged more than 106,000 reports of child pornography possession, creation, or distribution in 2004." Surprisingly, the NCMEC nevertheless puzzled over "why the totals have gone up remarkably each year."[10]

Many studies provide evidence that the teenage brain will neurochemically fuse fear and other toxic "gut reactions" with their sexual conduct. Neuroscientist Jack Fincher further explains:

[A]t first signs of danger the body systems reach "red-alert," with the cortex releasing the hypothalamus from inhibitory control, blood pressure increases, muscles tense, sensory perception increases, pupils dilate, pain awareness is reduced, the skin flushes, the hands become clammy, and the heart beats wildly in states of high sexual/fear, pornographically induced, arousal.

As a sexual or fear-based orgasm memory is awakened during pornography-induced anxiety, people imagine they are being sexually aroused by trigger sights. One is commonly aroused by a biological orgasm memory, fused with fear, shame, and the like.[11]

We also know that during coitus a neurochemical "bonding" hormone called oxytocin is triggered. Oxytocin works to attach the lovers more deeply to one another.[12] One's capacity for bonding is weakened by coitus with multiple partners or by repeated self-stimulation to pornographic images. This is the road to various problems, including impotence.

Sexual Abuse. Pornographically-triggered sibling abuse is extremely common. Dr. Victor Cline was commissioned by the U.S. Department of Justice to conduct a pilot field study on the effects of dial-a-porn on children (mostly pre-teens or early teens) who had been involved with pornography. Every child had become addicted.

> [W]ithout exception, the children (girls as well as boys) became hooked on this sex by phone and kept going back for more and still more ... One 12-year-old boy ... listened to dial-a-porn for nearly two hours ... A few days later he sexually assaulted a four-year-old girl in his mother's day care center. He had never been exposed to pornography before. He had never acted out sexually before and was not a behavior problem in the home. He had never heard of or knew of oral sex before listening to dial-a-porn. And this was how he assaulted the girl, forcing oral sex on her in direct imitation of what he had heard on the phone.[13]

Alongside the testimony of thousands of pornography's erototoxin victims, we can place the academic research. Here are just a few of the many scholarly studies documenting pornography's relation to sexual abuse:

- A 1987 study found that women who were battered, or subjected to sexual aggression or humiliation, had partners who viewed "significantly more pornography than" that of a "mature university population."[14]

- A 1995 meta-analysis found that violent pornography [did] reinforce aggressive behavior and negative attitudes toward women.[15]
- In a U.S. study of teenagers exposed to hard-core pornography, "Two-thirds of the males and 40 percent of the females reported wanting to try out some of the behaviors they had witnessed. And 31 percent of males and 18 percent of the females admitted doing some of the things sexually they had seen in the pornography within a few days after exposure."[16]
- A 1987 panel of clinicians and researchers concluded that "pornography's erototoxins stimulate attitudes and behavior that lead to gravely negative consequences for individuals and for society, and that these outcomes impair the mental, emotional, and physical health of children and adults."[17]
- A 1993 study found, "Exposure to sexually stimulating materials may elicit aggressive behavior in youth who are predisposed to aggression. Sexually violent and degrading material elicits greater rates of aggression and may negatively affect male attitudes toward women."[18]
- A 1984 evaluation of the increase in rape rates in various countries bears close correlation to the liberalizing of restrictions on pornography.[19]
- Three separate studies demonstrate that exposure to violent pornography [did] increase males' laboratory aggression toward women.[20]

In 1985, Dr. Judith Reisman, at the conclusion of her U.S. Department of Justice study, "Images of Children, Crime and Violence in *Playboy*, *Penthouse* and *Hustler*" (1985, 1989) states: "We found that in all three sex magazines, children were systemically described in cartoons, illustrations, photographs, and text as appropriate sexual targets for the reader/consumer. This mindset percolated down into the next pornography-using generation. Although erototoxic maga-zines have lost circulation or collapsed, their impotence-producing imagery is now more invasive and reaches more children via the Internet and mainstream media."

Marital Dysfunction. The impact on the future marriages of our children cannot be underestimated. If, in fact, with 35 percent of the adults having core biblical beliefs right now, we end up with a 50 percent divorce rate, then what might the divorce rate possibly look like with only 4 percent of this new generation having strong biblical beliefs—and virtually no absolutes? We noted earlier that up to 90 percent of our young people see pornography online, with 80 percent seeing hard-core porn. What will this do for the health of their marital relationships? What will their home lives look like? And what kind of families will your grandchildren grow up in? I ask myself such questions daily, wondering how my daughter is going to find a young man for a husband—one who doesn't have a porn movie endlessly looping through his mind, forcing him to compare his wife to a celluloid fantasy.

And did you know that a common outcome of pornography use is heterophobia? It's the conscious or unconscious fear, distrust, and disappointment in the opposite sex. Here's the devastating result: heterophobia produces impotence. So now the porn user can't fully make "love" (versus making sex) with his chosen beloved, due to his dependence on the Impotence Industry and its products. And that dependence runs deep, commonly leading to reliance upon erectile dysfunction medications, use of prostitutes, visits to strip shows, escalation to sadistic and child pornography, use of drugs, perpetra-tion of criminal sexual abuse.

Researchers found that after exposing college men to many presentations of non-violent or "soft" erototoxins over only a six-week period, these formally "normal" college males:

I HAVE problems with my family because of bad decisions my dad made with another lady outside of marriage. When I bring it up to express my thoughts they yell at me and tell me to leave the past behind. If I try to seek help for the way I hold my emotions in they won't let me because they do not like my friends. they will not even let me talk to my pastor. I am forced to keep everything locked up inside. When I told my mother she told me that I was just a baby and that I needed to grow up and stop lying to people. I hate myself and my family and it starting to get really bad where I just want to DIE and I even told my mother this and she just told me that I was a drama queen. I asked god for help but when it got worse then I had to stop myself from doing things that I knew was wrong and I eventually gave up on him. Then my Grandma got sick and died. I could not take it any more so I started to hurt myself. I could feel no emotional pain—I could not even bring one tear to my eye for my grandma's death I could only feel physical pain. I think what made me mad the most was that I wanted god's help but my mind or body or something would not let me receive it. I would ask god over and over to help me stop hurting myself but nothing is working and I still want to die so bad!!! All of my friends are here for me but my parents want to move because they say that my friends from church are just fakes that I should stop hanging with them. I cannot handle any of this. What am I to do?

- *Developed an increased callousness toward women, and would trivialize rape, while some rejected the idea that rape is a crime;*
- *Needed more deviant, bizarre, or violent types of pornography because normal sex no longer excited;*
- *Devalued marriage, doubted it would last, viewed having multiple sex partners as normal and healthy behavior.[21]*

Financial Drain. Since 1992, Big Pornography's erototoxic products are everywhere, with 58,200 children under the age of 18 kidnapped from our streets in 1999, most returning home sexually abused.[22] What was the monetary cost to taxpayers of tracking and finding and caring for these nearly 60,000 violated children? And what are the monetary costs in addressing the nearly two hundred other children kidnapped, raped, and killed each year? Also, the effects of erototoxins are reflected in the 418 percent increase in forcible rape and the 523 percent increase in unmarried births from 1960 to 1999.

All of these dismaying statistics translate not only into searing, heartbreaking human pain—they also point to the depletion of millions of your hard-earned dollars. Here are just three examples of the financial drain that comes with a sex-saturated society:

1. Teen mothers and their poverty. In the United States, the annual cost of teen pregnancies from lost tax revenues, public assistance,

all of these dismaying statistics translate not only into searing, heartbreaking human pain—they also point to the depletion of millions of your hard-earned dollars.

child health care, foster care, and involvement with the criminal justice system is estimated to be about $7 billion.[23] Pregnancy rates among adolescent females have fallen steadily in the past decade, from 116 per thousand female teens (ages 15 to 19) in 1990-1991, to 84 per thousand female teens in 2000. The vast majority of teen pregnancies (78 percent) are unintended.[24]

2. Abortions and their fees. More than one-third of all teenage pregnancies in the U.S. end in abortion.[25] Abortionists' fees for 45,014 abortions in the fiscal year of 1992-93 cost taxpayers $5,401,680. Costs were based on an average of $120 per abortion in the state of Missouri.[26]

3. STDs and their treatment. The annual comprehensive cost of sexually transmitted diseases in the United States is estimated to be well in excess of $10 billion.[27] Consider how young people are contributing to these horrific costs: The number of STD-infected 15 to 19 year olds has grown by 23 percent between 1996 and 2000.[28] Female adolescents, ages 15 to 19, have the highest incidence of both gonorrhea and chlamydia. And according to the latest CDC figures, 4 percent of new STD cases reported in 2000 occurred among 15 to 24 year olds.[29]

WHAT ARE THE MORAL AND SPIRITUAL IMPLICATIONS?

With all this pollution blowing through the minds of our young people, it's no wonder they have trouble deciding what's right or wrong. Without a strong moral foundation, how can they judge what to look at? Without clear standards coming through in their society and homes, how can they tell whether they should point-and-click or look away?

It's been said that Christian standards are simply a convenient means of judging others, a way to keep unenlightened and intolerant people "holier than thou." But as we can see, without a moral foundation, many aspects of our society begin to crumble, and our young people become the victims. Without standards, young people will listen to any music, watch any video, go to any Internet site. And their confusion will continue to spiral out of control.

For many teens, sexual involvement begins with being teased by the seemingly harmless innuendoes filling our "wholesome family programs." Young people who are sexually involved then begin to feel shame. They are embarrassed before God, because in many cases they had promised to wait for marriage. They feel like failures, having failed themselves, their God, and their parents. Now they walk around with a sense of impurity, even though they may believe God has forgiven them. They just haven't forgiven themselves.

Some are embarrassed to come back to church, as if they're sporting a bright scarlet letter on their chests. They imagine a wall between them and other "good" people, between them and God. And those who do step back inside the church will likely experience repeated failures; the shame piles up with excruciating weight.

Others exposed to some form of "teasing" get involved in pornography, whether online or through videos, and find themselves in unrelenting addiction. At first they thought it was fun, an innocent activity for pleasure that wasn't hurting anyone. Now they are addicted and feel as if there's no hope. What a price to pay!

We're not dealing with a bunch of "dirty old men" hiding in the shadows with their smut. We're facing our children and our neighbor's children. Right out in the open they are constantly exposed to

we're not dealing with a bunch of "dirty old men" hiding in the shadows with their smut. we're facing our children and our neighbor's children.

society's garbage. The vast majority of these young people are looking back at us with pleading eyes. They wish they could walk away. They look for a helping hand.

Don't our youth have a right to grow up in a clean environment? Don't I have the right to take my daughter to the mall without somebody's lingerie "secret"—and crude vision of womanhood—being imprinted on her brain? Shouldn't our teens have a chance for a healthy marriage and a wholesome family? It's time for us to make sure they have that opportunity. We must move from understanding the crisis to recognizing our need for a battle plan.

1 Rod Blagojevich's crusade is described in a *Time* magazine article, "Video Vigilantes," January 10, 2005, pp. 62-63. Quotes are from the article.

2 William J. Bennett, quoted in an article by Jim Fredricks, "Cat in the Hat," Houston Community Newspapers Online, 12/10/03. Available on the Web at: **www.hcnonline.com/site/news.cfm?BRD=1574&dept_id=532225&newsid=10607974&PAG=461&rfi=9**.

3 Quoted from the Commercial Closet, a gay-oriented Web site at **http://www.commercial-closet.org/cgi-bin/iowa/portrayals.html?record=719**.

4 Statistics from the Heritage Foundation Web site in a footnoted article, "Sexually Active Teenagers Are More Likely to Be Depressed and to Attempt Suicide," by Robert E. Rector, Kirk A Johnson, and Lauren R. Noyes, Center for Data Analysis Report #03-04. June 3, 2003. **http://www.heritage.org/Research/Family/cda0304.cfm#_ftn1**.

5 Chap Clark, *Hurt: Inside the World of Today's Teenagers* (Grand Rapids, MI: Baker Academic, 2004), p. 123.

6 Ronald Rolheiser, *The Holy Longing* (New York: Random House, 1999), p. 5.

7 A.R. Luria in Daniel Goleman and Richard Davidson, Eds., *Consciousness, Brain, States of Awareness, and Mysticism*. Harper & Row, New York, 1979, at 10.

8 Pasko Rakic, Science, Vol 294, "Enhanced: Neurocreationism—Making New Cortical Maps," November 2, 2001, at 1024-5.

9 Patrick Carnes, *Out Of The Shadows: Understanding Sexual Addiction*, Minneapolis Minn.: CompCare, 1983.

10 John Foley, *InternetWeek*, January 11, 2005, on the Web at: **http://www.internetweek.com/story/showArticle.jhtml?articleID=57700627**.

[11] The Psychopharmacology of Pictorial Pornography Restructuring Brain, Mind & Memory & Subverting Freedom of Speech. Judith Reisman, PhD. July 2003. **http://drjudithreisman.com/brain.pdf+The+Psychopharmacology+of+Pictorial+Por nography+Restructuring+Brain,+Mind+%26+Memory+%26+Subverting+Freedom+of +Speech+&hl=en&start=1&client**

[12] Oxytocin is released by genital stimulation in males and females and is implicated in sexual and maternal behaviors. Cornell University, **http://instruct1.cit.cornell.edu/courses/bionb424/students/nzl1/Oxytocin.htm**

[13] Peters, op.cit.

[14] E.K. Sommers and Check, J.V. Violence and Victims 1987, pp 2: 189-209. For full documentation of research cited here see, Peter Stock, "The Harmful Effects on Children of Exposure to Pornography," Canadian Institute for Education on the Family, November, 2004. **http://www.cief.ca/research_reports/harm.htm**.

[15] M. Allen, and D'Allessio, A meta-analysis summarizing the effects of pornography II: Aggression after exposure. Human Communication Research, 1995, pp. 22, 258-283.

[16] Jennings Bryant, "Report to Attorney General Commission on Pornography," U.S. Dept. of Justice, 1986.

[17] C. Everett Koop, "Report of the Surgeon General's Workshop on Pornography and Public Health." *American Psychologist.* 1987 Oct. Vol. 42 (10), pp. 944-945.

[18] Schimmer, R, "The impact of sexually stimulating materials and group care residents: A question of harm." *Residential Treatment for Children and Youth,* 11, 1993, pp.37-55.

[19] Court, J.H. "Sex and violence: a ripple effect." In N. Malamuth and E. Donnerstein, eds., *Pornography and Sexual Aggression* (New York: Academic Press, 1984).

[20] The four studies include two by Donnerstein:
   • Edward Donnerstein, "Aggressive Erotica and Violence Against Women." *Journal of Personality and Social Psychology,* Vol. 39, No. 2, 1980, pp. 269-277.
   • Edward Donnerstein, and Berkowitz, L. "Victim reactions in aggressive-erotic films as a factor in violence against women." *Journal of Personality and Social Psychology,* 1981, 41: 710-724.
   • Neal Malamuth. "Erotica, aggression and perceived appropriateness." Paper presented at the 86th annual convention of the American Psychological Association, Toronto, Canada, 1978.
   • Jennings Bryant, "Report to Attorney General Commission on Pornography," U.S. Dept. of Justice, 1986.

[21] Dolf Zillman and Jennings Bryant, "Pornography's Impact on Sexual Satisfaction." *Journal of Applied Social Psychology,* 1988: vol 18, no. 5, pp 438-453; and Zillman and Bryant, "Effects of Prolonged Consumption of Pornography on Family Values." *Journal of Family Issues:* vol. 9, No. 4, Dec. 1988, pp 518-544.

[22] See **drjudithreisman.org**, White Papers on the FBI and DOJ reduction of child sexual abuse reports and the National Center for Missing and Exploited Children data on child kidnapping.

[23] "Teen Pregnancy" on Women's Health Channel.

[24] Child Trends Data Bank, "Teen Pregnancy," 6/8/04.

[25] Child Trends Data Bank, "Teen Abortion," 6/8/04.

[26] "$5 Million Taxpayer's Dollars Paying Morgentaler's Rent," by Judi McLeod with files from Frank Kennedy.

[27] "Sexually Transmitted Diseases." A lecture by Dr. Neal R. Chamberlain.

[28] Child Trends Data Bank.

[29] "Friends, Friends with Benefits, and the Benefits of the Local Mall," *New York Times,* 5/30/04.

CHAPTER SIX

from understanding to action: the battle plan

Imagine living in London as Hitler marches across Europe. Every day you hear the reports of more fallen territory—Poland, Czechoslovakia, the Netherlands, and even France—all succumbing to the grinding German war machine. Soon there are 500,000 enemy soldiers stretched across the vast landscape of northern Europe. Now only 21 miles away, Nazi troopers eye your precious island across a narrow channel. You are left to the screaming air-raid sirens, running for cover into dark and damp subway tunnels.

The enemy seems invincible. You feel powerless. How do you fight back? Where do you even start?

The odds seem insurmountable, but Roosevelt and Churchill refuse to accept defeat. Instead, they develop a plan. After looking at all possible angles, they construct the largest and most comprehensive counteroffensive of the war.

Their strategy becomes the turning point, an overwhelming response from which Hitler never recovers—150,000 men invading with planes, parachutes, and boats of all sorts along a 50-mile stretch of beach in Normandy. Commencing battle in the early morning hours of June, 6, 1944, the 5,000 boats, 1,500 tanks, two million tons of ammunition, and 11,000 Allied aircraft all work together in a perfectly coordinated effort. First the high-flying bombers, then thousands of paratroopers dropping like flies from the sky. Then the landing craft filled with men and equipment.

They keep coming and coming and coming. By July, a million Allied soldiers are staged for battle in the north of France.

This was no half-hearted slap on the wrist to scold a "mean guy" for impolite behavior. This was a battle for civilization. The world was at stake. Without a thorough, well-planned response, a power-intoxicated tyrant would rule the future.

Are we in any less danger now?

STEP-BY-STEP COUNTERINVASION

The forces of the media do seem all-powerful and unstoppable, don't they? Yet it's been said that the journey of a thousand miles always starts with the first step. Yes, the road ahead is difficult. We can't accomplish everything all at once. We can't expect to arrive at our cherished destination—a healthy and wholesome youth culture in a day or two. But we can begin. Now.

Just as the Allied forces needed a plan, so do we. I'm offering a model, a simple but aggressive progression of four steps to re-take all the lost territory. The steps don't need to be linear; once hearts are captured, all three of the others can proceed simultaneously. But if adopted and followed, I believe this counteroffensive strategy will lead to profound, restorative change.

#1 Capture their hearts. We can't win a "culture war" just by fighting the evil forces in our society. We can't argue or debate our way to changing trends in beliefs. We must capture the hearts of young people. However, this can't be just a fancy recruiting ploy to get them in the door so they'll sign up for another church program. It must go much deeper and broader than that.

This is why holding large events is so important. At mega-events bringing teens together from across the nation, kids are able to "temporarily suspend disbelief" long enough to see how relevant the Bible is to their lives. This is also why youth pastors and parents must be trained and equipped (and why churches must change their methods and messages) to appeal to a new generation.

#2 Establish a beachhead. Once their hearts have been captured by God, we must help them build a beachhead—a groundwork, a firm spiritual foundation for a new lifestyle. The only way to see deep, long-term change in millions of young people is to get them deeply rooted in the foundations of the faith. This is the only way they will stay strong amidst the ravages of culture or the godless philosophies in their schooling.

This is about radically reversing the disheartening statistics we've seen in previous chapters. It's about building an army of young people well-established in what they believe and why they believe it. We won't be producing more nominal, illiterate Christians. In the process, they'll need to discover truth for themselves rather than passively accepting what has been preached to them or passed down from their parents. To accomplish this, church leaders, parents, and lay people will need to be available to walk young people through excellent discipleship materials.

MY MOM is an alcoholic and she is a mean drunk, and so dad never comes home. And people are starting to not believe i fell and walked into walls, when i come in with another black eye. But i don't know what to do, cause i don't want to betray her by telling someone and last time I did she broke my cheekbone, but it was an accident. She doesn't mean to do it she just does. she trusts me and i don't want to hurt her. What should I do? Any prayers would be helpful. — *Lauren*

#3 Develop esprit de corps. A firm sense of belonging is crucial to young people. Community is vital because teens need fellowship that's wedded to accountability. Deep inside, they want to feel they're part of something bigger than themselves—something substantive. This requires both local community and global community— a national (or international) family of teens connected primarily via the Web, but brought together in small and large gatherings—where the work of youth pastors and parents is strengthened and reinforced.

#4 Enter the fight. Assume we now have a massive community of teens whose hearts have been captured by God, who are rooting their souls down deep in His word, and who are connected with one another at a local and global level. Now imagine the impact if these teens were more than a community. Suppose they were an army actively engaged in changing their culture and their government. Suppose they were reaching out with the love of Jesus in their cities around the world. The potential impact upon our nation—and the world—is enormous.

In this simple model, every caring adult can be involved in rescuing our young ones. During World War II we came together for victory. Men went off to battle after waiting in lines for hours to enlist. Any who couldn't go still intensely engaged in the war. The women filled vacant factory jobs. Factories switched from producing tractors to rolling thousands of tanks off the assembly lines. Every citizen sacrificed and lived on rations in order to get the job done. Each person found his or her assignment, knowing it would take all of us together to defeat the enemy. Can we do any less for this generation?

"But what can I do, Ron?"

Can you love?

Can you pray?

Can you bring a few extra teens to church with your own? Can you smile at the door of the youth room as kids arrive? Can you go on teen outings to help the youth pastor? What are you willing to sacrifice to rescue a generation caught in a burning car?

We must turn our churches into hospitals for a broken-hearted generation, and it is not our youth pastor's job. It is not even our pastor's job. It's not the Sunday school teachers' job or the traveling youth evangelist's job.

It is our job. All of us—the body of Christ—must see the urgency and take action. The battle plan includes you.

PHASE I:
FORMING A UNIFIED NATIONAL FORCE

How is it that those who care dearly about the Spotted Owl cry out until they are heard? Those who want to "save the Earth" speak

the potential impact upon our nation—and the world—is enormous.

out until laws finally protect rivers and lakes. Now it is time to speak out to protect the hearts and minds of our young ones.

Throughout history, Christians have risen with a unified voice when their societies blatantly violated wholesome Judeo-Christian values. When our culture-shapers begin immersing us in depravity, we have an absolute obligation to raise our voices. Loudly. Until we are heard.

What if people from every stream of life came together with a unified message for our day? What if leaders from the business community, the entertainment world, the sports world, and politics all spoke with one clear voice? If we all came together as a Battle Cry Coalition, the voices of God-fearing people could encircle this young generation to show them the vast number of adults who care deeply for them.

Many are coming together already on **www.battlecry.com**. (Why not take a moment to go there and see for yourself?) Already momentum is building for the idea. This coalition is uniting to accomplish three main goals:

1. *Provide new updates on what is happening with today's teens, so you can pray more effectively;*
2. *Offer downloadable tools and resources for effectively reaching out to the teens in your region;*
3. *Be the voice of concerned adults all over the country who want to rescue this generation.*

What if millions of parents and grandparents united as one voice to say the same thing? Even teens themselves are uniting to take their own generation back. Battle Cry for a Generation is amassing teens by the thousands with the goal of 10 million voices, within four years, all standing for truth, decency, and a wise show of restraint in what is publicly available and destroying their peers. They are uniting to say, "We don't want you to wreck our generation any more!"

Some adults have even talked of starting a massive class-action lawsuit aimed at those destroying our kids' minds and hearts without claiming any responsibility. Similar lawsuits have apparently convinced the tobacco industry to stop aiming at our teens. And some of the more bold politicians may decide to walk down the forbidden path of legislation that protects our kids from media terrorists.

You may remember the story of William Wilberforce from a history class. He was a nineteenth-century Christian who refused to remain silent about slavery in England. His persistence paid off as finally England outlawed slavery just before he died in 1833. Like Wilberforce, we cannot allow the shapers of culture to shape it in a deadly direction any more.

PHASE 2:
FIGHTING ON THE LOCAL BATTLE FRONT

The remaining chapters of this book will be specific and practical, laying out exactly how each of us can be involved in the battle. Each of the groups below will have a whole chapter dedicated to it. For now, let's do a roll call and review the troops.

A. Enrolling the pastors and church leaders. Even as the prophet Malachi exhorted us, God wants to "turn the hearts of the fathers to their children, and the hearts of the children to their fathers" (4:6). The fathers of the faith, our pastors and church leaders, must take the lead if we are to have a hope of reaching this generation. Whatever the pastor emphasizes becomes the priority of the church.

If Roosevelt and Churchill had not felt the importance of Normandy, none of the troops would have been convinced it was worth the sacrifice. Making these teens a priority in our hearts is the first objective. Keeping them in the forefront of our minds until real change occurs is the next challenge. It cannot be a passing fad in

the devil's youth group is still bigger than all the rest of ours combined, so let's go to those no one else wants.

ministry. These pages cannot be a compelling read that you quickly forget. Our leaders must act to fully engage our congregations and keep them involved in reaching out to teens.

Thankfully, God is raising up leaders who really do care about youth ministry. A variety of national ministry leaders has contacted me after seeing a stadium full of young people on television. Watching the teens stream forward to give their lives to Jesus, these leaders have called to ask what they can do to help us reach even more. I have been moved by pastors of large and small churches across the country, those who are rising to the challenge and putting lots of money into local youth centers. They long to reach out to the hurting teens in their area.

By joining the Battle Cry Coalition and taking a stand, they are signing their names on the line—publicly. They are proving that it's not just MTV going after this generation. They realize war has been declared on this generation, and they have decided to risk a massive counteroffensive in the power of the Spirit, a blow that the enemy will never forget.

B. Strengthening trained youth workers. I have spent the last 18 years preaching my heart out to teenagers and equipping youth pastors to continue to build a strong youth ministry. Most of these youth workers desperately want to reach the teens in their community. But they are stopped in their tracks by the apathy of their local church lay people and leaders. Uninspired churchgoers often just want things to stay the same. They prefer the status quo to a bunch of those wild kids in "our church."

But whose church is it anyway? Is it ours, or Christ's?

Knowing that the pastor and people are now behind them, though, a new generation of youth workers can rise to the challenge of planning and reaching the teens in their regions. They'll do some deep thinking and planning, asking: "Exactly which teens are we called to reach, and how are we going to reach them?"

This is not a time to simply compete with the church down the street. If we all reach the kids we are called to reach, then we will reach them all. We ought to rejoice when kids fill the youth rooms of other churches; that can only help the kids in our own church. Together, let's go get the ones yet to be reached. The devil's youth group is still bigger than all the rest of ours combined, so let's go to those no one else wants.

For too long we have been content with spending time on Wednesdays with teens who belong to the parents attending our church. The pastor and parents are placated, so we think we've done our job. Some leaders think that no matter what they do, only 10 teens will ever come. So they think, "God only has 10 kids for me." Or they'll frame it in theological terms and say, "I am not into quantity but quality; after all, Jesus only had 12 disciples."

Jesus did not die for 12 quality people. Striving to reach all the teens in your region doesn't mean you don't want them to grow into mature Christians. In order to get both, we must emphasize both and insist on it. Many thriving youth ministries all over the country are doing just that. Chapter 9 will tell you all about it.

C. Engaging the footsoldiers. Lay people—especially parents—are the key to reaching all 33 million youth caught in the crossfire. The false comfort of paying our tithes and then going home will no longer suffice. Soldiers are willing to endure personal hardship for the greater cause.

The footsoldiers need to be regularly motivated, sufficiently equipped, and then deeply immersed in a specific duty that is worthy of their volunteer time. Once they have finally realized that throwing up their hands in futility isn't a Christian option, they must see the actual options for their involvement. In Chapter 10 you will find numerous examples of what others are doing to get involved and make a difference.

D. Filling all the support roles. In any military offensive, support roles are crucial. The battle is hardly limited to the front lines. The soldiers must be fed, and they must be continually supplied with the tools and weapons they need to overcome the enemy. This demands unfailing hard labor behind the lines. In Chapter 11, we'll see how it's done.

TAKING BACK THE TERRITORY, ONE REGION AT A TIME

Just as in a natural war, it is not possible to win a supernatural war overnight. A wise general will plan, city by city, how he is going to take a nation. In an effort to take back their generation, region by region, local leaders are targeting several urban metroplexes each year, hoping to make deep and lasting impact in teens' lives and in the regions where they live.

To demonstrate that students can affect their own generation, we are partnering with churches in several regions each year. In each of these metroplexes we are encouraging all the churches to join in bringing the most unreached teens along with their youth groups to a stadium in their region for a massive event. The focus of the event will be evangelism and evangelism training.

In advance, we train the youth pastors in a philosophy of

ministry that helps them catch all the fruit that is harvested. This also prepares them to take action after the event. As the teens leave the event, they are fully motivated and equipped to go and invade their generation with the Gospel of Jesus for the next year.

In the year following the massive event, we will keep the youth groups tied together through the Internet in order to help them fuel each others' fire. We want all youth groups to double and triple during the course of the year. We want every group involved in acts of service in their communities, not just getting together for fun. We will monitor the teen pregnancy rate, teen drug use, and teen violence. Then we plan to meet back in the same stadium the following year to celebrate all that God has done during that year. We can then show the world the data—proving that teens can indeed change their generation.

We will proclaim that the Bible does work—that changing the heart changes the actions—all of which changes the social trends on a grand scale. In fact, over a hundred thousand young people have already signed their name to this document:

THE TEENAGE BILL OF RIGHTS

We, a new generation of young Americans, in order to protect the heritage of our forefathers and secure the blessings of liberty for ourselves and generations to come, do affirm and pledge this declaration.

When character and morality are uncommon qualities,
When corporations and marketers seek to profit from our destruction,
When pop culture icons do not represent our values,
When Judeo-Christian beliefs are labeled as intolerant,
When activists seek to remove God from our schools,

When truth is deemed relative and unknowable,

It is necessary for us, the emerging generation of young
Americans, to stand for what is right and reclaim the values
that have made our nation great. We call our nation to a higher
standard, a lifestyle based

not on convenience, but on character,

not on what is easy, but what is excellent,

not on what feels good, but what is good,

not on popularity, but on principle,

not what is tempting, but what is true.

We, as young Americans, assert our right to determine our future
and the future of our great nation. We hold these truths as our
God-given rights, and we embrace them with our hearts and our
lives:

We recognize that God, our Creator, is the source of all truth.

We will live with honor, always striving to do the right thing, even
when it is unpopular.

We will be honest and truthful in matters large and small,
regardless of the consequences.

We will take responsibility for our actions, and not point to government, schools, celebrities, parents, or friends to justify our
wrong decisions. We recognize that we are responsible for our
mistakes.

We will pursue purity throughout our lives. We will not be seduced
by a fabricated idea of sex and love. We will save our bodies and
hearts for our future spouse, and once married, we commit to
pursue faithful and enduring relationships.

We will see through the lies of drugs and alcohol and refuse to let
any chemical influence our thinking or destroy our lives.

We will respect the authorities placed in our lives, even though
some may not live as honorably as they should. We will honor
our parents, teachers, and other leaders.

We will reach out with compassion to the hurting and less

fortunate, both in our society and around the world. We refuse
to be absorbed with our own comforts and desires.
We recognize the value of each life, whether born or unborn, and
we seek to protect those who are unable to protect themselves.
We will do our best to represent and communicate our Creator
to our peers, leaders, and society as a whole. We will work to
see that every person has the opportunity to see and hear about
the true nature of our God.

In signing, we commit to pursue a life that exemplifies these
standards. We refuse to sit idly by and witness the destruction of
our generation. With God's help, we envision a bright and
prosperous future for the nation we love.

The thousands of young people making these promises are
proclaiming their right to set the standard for their generation. Do you
know a youth group that ought to make the same commitment? But
they can't do it alone. In Part III ahead, we'll see just how much they
need our helping hand.

the rescue

Lifeguard Rob Howes and three teenagers, one of whom was his daughter, Niccy, were swimming out to sea at Ocean Beach in New Zealand when seven bottlenose dolphins sped towards them and herded them together.[1] Why? Because the swimmers were under a great white shark attack. "It glided around in an arc and headed for the other two girls," the veteran lifeguard said. "My heart went into my mouth, because one of them was my daughter."

But thank God for those dolphins and their circle of protection! In this final portion of the book, we'll see the need to form a similar type of barrier between our teens and the cultural "sharks" circling them.

The good news is that the Bible offers many practical answers to the question we often raise: "But what can I do?" We'll look at some answers for pastors, youth pastors, parents, grandparents, business people, and twenty-somethings. We *all* have a role to play.

CHAPTER SEVEN

leaders arise!

"The preaching of my senior pastor."

This was 15-year-old Amber's response when I asked her about her experience in youth group. First she told me how hard it had been to find a group where other teens were seriously committed to growing in the Lord. "In my last youth group, kids would leave the worship service early and go smoke and cuss behind the church," she said. "I finally found another church with a youth group only 10 miles away."

These two churches had lots of similarities—same size, same demographics, same theological perspectives. So I asked Amber for a deeper analysis, since teens excel at going right to the heart of a matter. "So, Amber," I asked. "Why do you think your new youth group is filled with teens who really love God and your old youth group was full of kids who smoke pot and mock the worship services?" That's when, after pondering for several minutes, she gave her thoughtful and poignant response. *"It is the preaching of my senior pastor."*

even if you don't feel you relate to today's teens very well, your role in their lives is more important than you may think.

Does this surprise you as much as it did me? I talk with teens all the time. I would have thought Amber might say something about the preaching of the youth pastor, or the state of the youth room, or the activities in the youth program. But no. She spoke about an adult function in her church. Her 15-year-old mind was quite astute. She easily realized that the senior pastor set the tone for the spirit of the entire church, including the youth ministry.

I continued exploring this with Amber. "What is it about your senior pastor's preaching that makes the difference?" She remarked that "he seems to take us more seriously as teens; his teaching is deep from the Bible, and this helps us all keep growing."

ARE YOU PARTIALLY PASTORING?

Suppose you are the senior pastor. Even if you don't feel you relate to today's teens very well, your role in their lives is more important than you may think. Consider the experience of Willie George, senior pastor of Church on the Move in Tulsa, Oklahoma. He tells of his frustration after having gone through several different youth ministers in just a couple of years. He was "between youth pastors" once again, trying to find a dedicated worker who would really stick.

After much struggle, he finally came to a profound realization that changed his whole approach to church ministry. He put it like this: "I need to pastor the entire church, not just the adults."

As a result of his new insight, he made some changes. He decided, for example, to be the interim "youth pastor" while the search for a permanent minister continued. He began praying with the adult and teen leaders and began attending the youth group meetings every Wednesday night. He got to know the kids by name. He listened to them, taught them, and asked God for His plan for this youth ministry.

Pastor George had been very successful as a senior pastor, with thousands attending his services every Sunday. Yet his youth ministry seemed to flounder no matter which "dynamic" individual he would bring on staff. The résumé of each new youth pastor was always more impressive than the last. But the ministry just wouldn't grow.

Finally, as Pastor George began to focus on the youth and get God's heart for this part of his flock, a rather miraculous transformation kicked in. Momentum began to build. Teens started bringing their friends. And George developed a theme and vision for what this youth ministry in his church could be. When he finally did hire a person to fill the role of youth pastor, he found someone to finish building the vision for teens that he had developed. After the three months he spent with the young people in his flock, not only did he have a sincere heart of love for them, they felt valued by him. Today thousands attend his youth ministry each week.

Realizing that being a pastor means *shepherding all the people in your church* is a great beginning. These young people are a part of your flock. They are your sheep. And they desperately need the

I'M GAY. or at least I think I might be. I'm afraid my church won't accept the kind of person I am. I am very confused. Does God love me still? I'm scared I'm doing something wrong by loving someone who is my own sex. No one pushed me into it. It just happened and I'm scared. I can't help it. I'd like to find a group of people who are struggling as much as I am. —Ro

"Fathers [of the church] to turn their hearts" toward the younger generation. As leaders, when we embrace these kids as our God-given responsibility, the questions about "what to do with them" quickly receive clear answers.

While it's true that senior pastors can't single-handedly do everything required to run an effective church, there are some things they just can't allow others to carry. A heart for the plight of teens in America is one of them. *We can't subcontract our love for teenagers.*

We've seen that cultural wolves have broken into the fold, and the sheep are running confused and scared. These sheep, especially the young, are starkly vulnerable. They have no idea of the wolves' devouring ferocity. We, as pastors and leaders, are called to lay down our lives for these precious sheep. Yes, we may have other shepherds in the pen helping us. But when there is imminent danger, we ourselves must jump to the rescue. This is the essence of shepherding.

Knowing these things is the first step toward meaningful intervention. We can change the direction of this generation if we, as leaders, take our legitimate shepherding responsibilities seriously . . . and personally. Yes, we wonder, what can be done against all the forces of the techno-terrorists? What can be done to prevent the prince of darkness from stealing the soul of an entire generation? But if you, as a pastor, are seriously asking such questions, then the enemy is surely trembling.

Where do we start? At the most basic level, the massive armies called the body of Christ must be alerted to the crisis. Your youth pastor cannot do it alone. He or she must know there is a senior pastor and a whole local church standing with them. What does that mean? Standing with them means much more than just hollering encouragement from across the parking lot as parents drop off their teens for youth group.

Instead, leaders must engage the entire church in this crisis. When MTV wants to wreck a generation, it doesn't just hire one guy and say, "Hey, it's your job alone to go wreck a generation." An entire industry is built around pumping garbage into our kids. And they make a lot of money doing it. Similarly, we must fully engage every resource at our disposal.

You will come up with all kinds of creative ideas, strategies, methods, and approaches. But let me offer at least three over-arching principles to help guide you.

Make your church a hospital for a brokenhearted generation. Imagine a Sunday morning church service filled with all kinds of teenagers that you have never seen before. All different colors and backgrounds being apprehended by different members of your congregation and lavished with love. Imagine the grandparents in your

MY BEST FRIEND Elaine (19) was stabbed 15 times in the chest and smothered by her boyfriend. She was taken from me the only person who truly knew me. I felt so alone. After that I got so mad at God I thought how could he let this happen. God never gives u a situation u cant handle well I felt like I had enough. How could he let all this happen to me. I tried so hard to understand my life and the things that happened. Then not even a year after that my dad goes nuts after drinking all day and night and beats my mom up and tries to shoot us. We left with the clothes on our backs and moved as far away from Michigan as we could. It took him almost killing us for her to leave. I can't trust anyone. I can't sleep ... I'm broken. There is people around me but i feel so alone. I don't know I have no one to talk to about this and I just had to get some of it out. —*Tawnya* church loving these kids as their own grandchildren and taking them to lunch afterwards. Imagine parents who've refused to just bring their own kids to church but insisted on picking up the friends that their teens have invited.

Can you see it?

Imagine if all the church members actually took ownership of this generation and insisted on doing their part. This picture of the local church acting as an army medical hospital in a battle zone ... is within our reach. By the grace of God—and through the steady determination of pastors gripped by a heart for teens—we can do it.

Regularly touch your members' hearts with the plight of teens. Give your congregation enough information and stories about what is really happening until they begin to weep for teenage souls. We must not simply reduce our presentations to statistics that depersonalize the real value of the souls at stake. By inserting stories in the weekly bulletin, showing videos on the current struggles of teens, and inviting teens to share testimonies on a regular basis in church services, you can begin to woo the hearts of your adults. Click on **www.battlecry.com** for resources to do this.

Knowing national statistics, and how your local community compares to them, will help bring perspective. But the goal is to monitor those local stats and plan how to beat them. Possibly having every member of your congregation read this book would help. (Bulk orders from the publisher are being made available at discounted rates. All profits will go toward reaching more teens, not to the author. Call toll free: 1-800-323-7543. Use the book and the study guides in Sunday school classes for adults, cell groups, and Bible studies to strengthen the commitment to teens and understanding of their plight.)

This effort must go far beyond just one sermon, or even one series of sermons. For the next three or four years, we must passionately and regularly paint a picture of teenage America for our congregations to use as food for prayer and action. (Go to **www.battlecry.com** to find sermon outlines and tools that will visually engage your congregation to have a heart for teens.)

Help your adults find their assignments in the battle.
Once you have established the urgency in their hearts, it is time to engage them in the fight. In a very real sense our churches must become an emergency ward for teens who are bruised and bloodied from the battle. We, as Christians, must all be engaged in the triage necessary to rescue them, one by one. Each person has a role to play in reaching this generation.

Church members find their assignments as we give them practical opportunities to be involved, to "try on" new ministries to see how they fit. At first maybe only a few of the faithful will commit to one of the assignments you have made available. As they begin to see fruit, be sure to have them testify publicly in order to encourage others to engage. Bottom line: regularly give your congregation a chance to understand God's love for teens, then to respond with their own loving actions.

WILL YOU INVEST IN THIS GENERATION?
It's easy to talk about reaching a generation for Christ. But if we are to reach them, we must put our money where our mouth is. That is, let's put our money where our hearts are. It will cost money. If we value teens, we will spend money on them. Today's teens feel valued

> it's easy to talk about reaching a generation for Christ. but if we are to reach them, we must put our money where our mouth is.

senior pastor, your youth workers desperately need your encouragement, support, and strength. they need you to be the champion of the cause for reaching this generation.

by the world because the world invests in them. Will we do less than the secular marketers?

It will cost to have an engaging youth room and a van to get them there. It will cost to have tools and curriculum to teach the truths of God's Word in a contemporary manner so they'll listen and respond. It will cost to hire a youth pastor and other youth workers to spend all their time rescuing those caught in the crossfire.

Rather than thinking, "But what will I get for this investment?" let's look at it a little differently. We know that teens won't be the biggest givers right now. But they are better than no givers in the future (which is what we may have if we don't reach this generation).

If we do think of return-on-investment, we might end up concluding that teens actually are the best investment. (I'm speaking of eternal returns, of course.) True, they may not recoup the money you spend at the moment. But if you calculate the souls-per-dollar ratio, and the closed-up heart of the average adult ... perhaps the kids are worth selling the farm. (After all, as we have already seen, 77 percent of those who come to the Lord do so before the age of 21.[2])

So how much to invest? Some pastors use John 20 as a guide. Jesus urged Peter: "If you love me, feed my lambs." The next two times He said "feed my sheep and take care of them." Since Jesus specifically referred to "lambs" in this final exhortation before He left, no doubt we should pay attention to our lambs too. If Jesus emphasized lambs 33 percent of the time, then maybe we should invest accordingly. Some churches then invest, as a matter of principle, 33 percent of all their revenue in their children's and youth ministries. Not a bad guideline, especially considering the urgency of the moment.

NOW FOR THE YOUTH PASTOR'S PERSPECTIVE . . .

Spending years on the road motivating and training youth pastors, I have frequently encountered a vexing reality. Many youth pastors have told me, on occasions too numerous to count, of the absolute devastation of their passion to reach teens. The cause? The devastating discouragement flowed in as a result of talking to their senior pastor.

Many return home from an inspiring conference with the adrenaline pumping, with bubbly zeal—and some strategy—to make significant inroads into the local youth culture. Yet I have been told of senior pastors who nevertheless "pull the plug" on a youth ministry for money reasons—or simply because they (secretly?) don't want the youth ministry to outshine the adult ministry as it grows. Surely such senior pastors need to hear Jesus once again:

> Whoever welcomes a little child like this in my name welcomes me. But if anyone causes one of these little ones who believe in me to sin, it would be better for him to have a large millstone hung around his neck and to be drowned in the depths of the sea . . .
>
> See that you do not look down on one of these little ones. For I tell you that their angels in heaven always see the face of my Father in heaven. —Matthew 18:5-6, 10

Senior pastor, your youth workers desperately need your encouragement, support, and strength. They need you to be the champion of the cause for reaching this generation. (Don't get me wrong, they are willing to do the work. I have not seen many lazy youth workers; it's an oxymoron.)

The fact is, the largest youth groups in America now all seem to have at least one thing in common. They come in all shapes and sizes—different denominations, different theologies, and different philosophies of ministry. But the one uniting factor is that they have a senior pastor who really cares and is involved. He is investing into the next generation and keeping his congregation invested. When you invest in them, they know you care. And teens are always attracted to those who care about them.

The rest of this chapter is dedicated to giving you the youth pastor's perspective—raw and uncut, right off the street. I have included survey responses—comments and stories—from youth pastors all across the country. In these responses, you'll hear the heartbeat of your own youth pastor. You'll feel their dedication and their deep desire that you care and work with them to reach a generation under attack. In addition, you'll find a plethora of statements about what other senior pastors have done to make a huge difference for the teens of their church and their community. Read them and be inspired.

■■■■■■■

SURVEY QUESTION:

"WHAT DO YOU WISH YOUR SENIOR PASTOR KNEW ABOUT YOUTH MINISTRY?"

- I wish he knew how much his leadership really impacts the kids. Teens are really good at feeling one way and showing something else. They respect him and honor his leadership, but typically they do not reach out to him and show it.
- How seriously we are undermined and bad-mouthed by a handful in the congregation.
- I wish he didn't expect me to be in the office most of my salaried hours. A lot of times, I feel like I have to spend relationship-building time with teens on my own time, which can be overwhelming.
- LOL—the stress involved with ministering to youth; my need for an office/room for all my teaching aids and materials.
- That he realized unchurched youth do not behave like other members of the congregation. We can't be so "pious" that we scare them off.
- I wish he knew what effect traditional worship has on our church attendance.
- If only he knew how important he is in making the dreams of our youth ministry come true!
- That youth need love more than they need rules. "They won't care how much you know until they know how much you care." Also, youth ministry is much more effective in the one-on-one relationship than in meetings. This focus is often overlooked, but it should be a key element in youth ministry.
- The kids really do love seeing their senior pastors come to youth events. Some kids, regardless of their family's church involvement, have few adults showing interest in what they are doing.

Coming to youth activities proves that the senior pastors don't just say that they care; their actions make their words true.

- That his role as the senior pastor is to be the shepherd of the teens as well as the adults. He may lead through the youth pastor but has to have a connection of some sort with the youth ministry. He can't sit from afar and pat the youth pastor on the back and expect the youth ministry to feel a part of the overall church ministry.

- That it takes the entire church, not just the youth pastor and leaders, to make a youth ministry successful!

- That our budget should be proportional to the ministry needs we have. We barely have 10 percent of the budget but we are one of the largest ministries. We raise a great deal of our own money for various needs.

- I wish he knew that the stakes are higher now. Once we could "wait" to talk to kids about sex until high school. We can't wait that long now. And I wish that he knew that kids, while capable of totally moronic and stupid things, are also capable of changing the world. Really.

- How I wish Pastor knew how vital youth ministry is and that if we don't get these kids on fire for God now, while they are young, there is a good chance they will never be on fire adults. That youth ministry is not just a social club, a "safe" place for teens to hang out, but that it is an extremely important tool for changing people's lives forever!

- The importance of discipling the parents of my kids. Being more tough on the parents in encouraging them to be in the Word and working on their own relationship with Jesus. Just dropping their kids off at youth group isn't enough. He needs to realize that Youth Ministry is really about Family Ministry.

- Recognize that he turns the "head" of the church whichever way he likes. When the pastor is passionate about the youth, it shows!

I would like to see him at youth activities to encourage outreach in our community to the youth.

- I think he gets it. Our mid-week youth service grew from 25 to 250 in attendance. The growth came overnight and can be highly attributed to the fact that our senior pastor gave our youth ministry an increased budget, use of the sanctuary, extra staff support, and tons of publicity. God is Good!

SURVEY QUESTION:
"DO YOU HAVE A STORY ABOUT HOW GROWING YOUR YOUTH GROUP HAS GROWN YOUR CHURCH'S ADULT ATTENDANCE?"

- Over the past two years our youth ministry has exploded. We went from 30-40 kids every week to over 200 on a weekly basis. During this time, not only did we attract teens to our youth center, but we started to see teens at church on Sunday and Tuesday nights, along with their parents and brothers and sisters. We are continuing to grow ...

- Many of our kids' parents do not attend our church. Through the life-changing message of the Gospel, we've seen teens improve in their relationship with their parents. In turn, their parents have come to our church to see what's causing the change in their teen's life. A number of parents have told me, "Please keep doing what you are doing; it has made a tremendous impact on my teen." So youth ministry is definitely a strategy for church growth.

- Yeah! Quite a few families have joined our church via their kids coming to the youth ministry. I view our ministry as a port of entry into the rest of the church. I guess you could say that the parents see their kids being changed and loved on, and they want to check it out for themselves. Their thoughts might be, "If my kids are being taken care of spiritually, then I can be taken care of too."

- A testimony we heard last week from a father visiting our church for the first time was: "Last week I was so impressed to see the youth from your church involved in a community event that I said to myself, 'That is the kind of church we are looking for.'" He and his wife attended our church the following Sunday after the community event with their four kids, three of them teens.

- Our church began as a plant eight years ago. We started with a handful of people in a living room. We emphasized relationships and started with small groups right at the beginning. It was through these small groups that we started two youth cells. Since that time we have now built our own building, we have 75 youth in our church, and many of the parents of the youth are now going to our church, which is seeing a weekly attendance of over 450.

- Last year we began adult sponsorships of our youth. We made up information cards for each youth with their picture, name, address, school, and some of their interests listed. Unrelated adults were encouraged to choose a youth they would pray for throughout their time in Youth Fellowship. The adults could also form a closer relationship with that youth by giving birthday or other gifts, going to school events, or inviting the teen to dinner. The main responsibility of the adult is to pray for the youth. Kids also are informed of who their sponsors are and are encouraged to get to know them better. Several of the adults who participated last year did form new relationships with these kids.

- The three newest families to join our church began with their kids coming to youth group. Then the entire family began coming to church.

- He is constantly telling me he is "for me." He prays with me and for me and occasionally writes little letters of appreciation. Just today, I was walking to the youth room, and he passed me and said, "How is my Number One Youth Pastor?" He instills confidence in me, and my performance is empowered by that!

- He is always investing in my life as my pastor. He takes time every week to get together with me, not just to talk ministry, but to encourage me in my own walk with Christ. Also, last year he went with me to a youth conference that I'd wanted to attend for a few years.

- He prays for me and the rest of our lay team. Does a lot of the "behind the scenes" things that make the meetings run smoothly (photocopying, etc.). He attends our planning meetings and gives sound advice. Invites the youth band to play frequently at Sunday morning worship services.

- Taking the youth staff out to dinner, just to thank us, has been one of the most meaningful forms of encouragement from my pastors. They thanked us for all our hard work and gave us a time to talk about any concerns, frustrations, or new ideas. Another awesome time of encouragement from my pastoral staff came

he takes time every week to get together with me, not just to talk ministry, but to encourage me in my own walk with Christ.

LEADERS ARISE!

when they drove out to the youth's spring campout. The youth really wanted to rough it in the woods, so we did just that. We were up a long, winding logging road where the nights were cold and dark. The kids were having a blast, and one night, the senior pastor and associate pastor drove all the way out there just to participate in our evening campfire.

- My pastor meets with me at least once a month for lunch. He always starts our meeting by praying, of course, but then the first thing he says is, "Tell me everything." He sits intently while I fill him in on everything that has been going on. Before we finish up our meeting, he always asks me, "What can I do to help you?" This time with him reassures me about how vital the youth ministry is to this very overworked man of God. I have never had to wonder where he stood, or if he supported me. He tells me all the time.

- He's excited about the ministry and my involvement in it. He's helped me approach the church board to request funds and assistance on several occasions. He's helped us find funds to buy some youth Bibles for us to use at YG, found us donors for big financial needs, led mission trips (open to both youth and adults—occurring when I could not go along at all!).

- Our senior pastor views parents as the key youth pastors of their teens. He makes home visits with parents to work with them to better their parenting skills. He also attends each meeting and does a special breakout session with parents during this time. He takes time to get to know the teens and show his support for their involvement in church life and ministry.

- Recently, my senior pastor (who has three teenage sons in the youth group) encouraged me to share every detail of my dream for our youth ministry with him and the board. I'm encouraged to know that he wants to hear all about my "wish list!"

- Our pastor has set aside a Sunday evening every other month for the teens to be in charge of the service. He has me do the speaking so the congregation can get an idea of what the teens are learning and what issues they are facing. These services have really bridged the gap between old and young, giving the older people more respect for what we do.

SURVEY QUESTION:
"SHARE ABOUT SOMETHING YOUR PASTOR HAS DONE THAT SEEMED TO DISCOURAGE YOUR CHURCH'S YOUTH MINISTRY."

- Uuhmm ...
- As far as encouraging me ... Nada. Nil. Zip. Nothin'.
- He's supportive in word only.
- Wow! That is a hard one. He really doesn't do a great job in this area. He just says, "Keep it up."
- He hardly speaks to my wife or me concerning anything, much less youth ministry. We don't have staff meetings, and he never meets with us to discuss youth ministry. The only time he gets involved is when he wants an account of the money spent for youth trips or activities.
- He has not stepped up to support the youth ministry and make it a priority. We meet in a large kitchen next to the nursery and have not been able to decorate our room to fit the youth.
- He does nothing with youth. At this time I am very discouraged. And though I know God has put youth and their parents on my heart, I am no longer actively serving a youth ministry at this time.

■■■■■■■

Those final comments break my heart. How do they affect you, Pastor? I recall a cute little quip that really isn't very happy. It seems a mother was overheard talking about her teenage daughter: "She's very independent—she lives alone at our house." Sadly, many of our teens are living completely alone amidst our thriving and growing church families. Who will shepherd them?

[1] Shark story by Ainsley Thomson, 11/25/2004, on the Web at :
http://icelava.net/Forums/ShowPost.aspx?PostID=816.
[2] Evangelism is Most Effective Among Kids, The Barna Group, Ltd., October 11, 2004.
http://www.barna.org/FlexPage.aspx?Page=Barna Update&BarnaUpdateID=172

CHAPTER EIGHT

CHAPTER EIGHT

releasing the generals

"So, what do you do for a living?"

"I'm in ministry."

"Oh, you're a pastor?"

"No ... I'm a youth pastor."

Add a sheepish look and a condescending stare to the brief conversation above and you've got a little drama that plays out regularly in church circles. The look on many peoples' faces when they discover someone is a youth minister often conveys something just short of contempt. Their reaction seems to say, "Oh, you're not a *real* minister; you don't work with *real* people."

To a large extent youth ministry is looked down upon. However, I believe this will change as we all realize that youth pastors are our generals in this offensive. They're the ones leading the battle to rescue a generation and return our nation to its rich heritage.

If they are to give heavily into the church youth ministry fund, the members must respect the leadership you bring to that ministry.

It has been said that wars are won by generals. Generals grasp the wishes and directives of their commander and know the conditions of the troops. They understand the enemy's strategies and creatively navigate through these to reach victory. They devise the battle plan and then see that it is executed. They can view the battlefield clearly and maneuver their troops into the best positions to conquer the enemy.

The Bible says in 1 Timothy 4:12, "Don't let anyone look down on you because you are young, but set an example for the believers in speech, in life, in love, in faith and in purity." Paul is exhorting us to not look down on those with strong faith simply because they are young. It follows, then, that we shouldn't look down on those who *work with the young*. For too long we have considered church youth workers as Christian babysitters for teens.

Note to the youth pastors (everyone else can skip this part):

Be careful not to do things that perpetuate the youth pastor stereotype. For example, when you attend church on Sunday, dress as an adult, not like the teens. "But I need to relate to the kids," you might say. Not on Sundays. You need to relate to the adults so they respect you and see you as a viable entity. Dress with the same decorum as your senior pastor does. Also be careful not to talk like a teenager if/when the pastor gives you a chance to preach or share announcements from the pulpit. And be sure not to wear any body piercings, purple hair, or temporary tattoos in Sunday worship.

Such behaviors inhibit your effectiveness in ministry. People will keep seeing you as an "overgrown teenager" rather than a well-equipped minister who's serious about reaching a generation. If they are to give heavily into the church youth ministry fund, the members must respect the leadership you bring to that ministry.

Some in youth ministry would persist and argue, "I just want to relate to the teens, and of course the adults will not understand how I dress or act." We have to be careful here, because this argument can be an excuse

LATELY, I've been really depressed. I just wish that I wasn't born. I want to commit suicide, but yet I don't. I don't get along with my sister and just feel like a failure. I've tried to be nicer to her, but I screw up every time and then get all down on myself. I just don't know what to do. Every goal I make, I screw up. I had promised myself I would write in my journal every day, I haven't in over a week. I wanted to read my Bible every day, but I always forget, or get too busy. I'm just a flat out failure! I feel so bad about myself. I have an awesome mom, an okay dad, a precious but annoying little brother, and a pesty sister. I just hate myself and I don't know why. I have a terrific youth pastor, I love her and go to her about all kinds of things, but I just can't about this and I don't know why. I need help! —*Hannah (14)* that we use to keep from having to act in a mature manner. Then we complain, "These parents never volunteer or give money to the youth ministry." But we've initiated a self-fulfilling prophecy and don't realize it. If they respect us, they will volunteer and give. They will follow us into battle.

Okay, now everyone can read again.

Youth pastors are specialists in reaching those whom no one else has given much hope. They are experts in catching a generation as it slips on the cultural banana peel off the cliff into moral relativism. They are the ones catching kids no one else knows how to reach. When everyone else is saying, "I just don't know what to do with these strange creatures," youth pastors say, "Give them to me; I know what to do!" They are the ones God trusts with teens when they're most open to the Gospel. He has trusted them to lead and influence during some of the most moldable years of kids' lives. He trusts our youth pastors with the next generation of Christians.

It is a great privilege. And serious business.

IT'S MORE THAN GOOD FUN?

We all need to understand the role of a youth pastor who is destined to make a huge impact in this battle for a generation. This person will be quite different from the "status quo youth minister." His mind and heart are fueled by a sense of destiny. She knows she has a short window of opportunity (5-7 years, as we have seen) to act and so refuses to waste time just keeping Christian kids occupied with "good, clean fun."

Jesus didn't die so we could have good, clean fun. We can have that without Christ. Yes, you will have fun as a Christian, but that certainly isn't the goal. The goal is to find our place in God's purpose, to find our Kingdom assignment. When we find it, and pursue it with all our hearts, we take up the most incredible adventure that life can offer.

So, where does a youth specialist actually begin to make a huge impact? It seems there's so much to do that just thinking about it wears us down. And some of us have tried so many things (which haven't worked) that we're a bit disillusioned. We're the ones who pacify ourselves with, "I just want to love kids."

Who could argue with that? The question is, does your love for young people provoke you to take the appropriate actions? Of course we must sincerely love them, because they can smell a fake a million miles away. We know love breaks through all the barriers and "never fails." *So if we really do love them, let's go after them!*

- *Do we love them enough to methodically plan how to effectively reach the unreached in our city?*
- *Do we love them enough to think through how we are going to disciple them after they give their lives to Christ?*
- *Do we love them enough to do the lonely work of developing ourselves as mature Christian leaders so we can handle the ministry as it grows?*

we must become vision-driven and not just activity-driven. we can do activities until we have worn ourselves out and still not reach many kids— and not fulfill our destiny.

Jesus loves every one of them, so let's start dreaming as big as He does—and let Him do the math.

Loving them doesn't mean just hanging out with them, doing fun activities with them, or even having great ministry events and altar calls. It means carrying out a loving plan under a clearly defined philosophy.

WHAT IS YOUR PHILOSOPHY OF MINISTRY?

This is the heart of the matter. Many, maybe most, youth workers began their ministry at the bidding of a pastor who asked them to "volunteer to help out with the kids for a while." Now, five years later, you have such a growing love for them you could never quit. Inherent in that mindset is the thought, "I am here to take care of the kids whose parents attend this church."

This perspective is fine, to a point. But here's the downside: It makes reaching out to other kids "the right thing to do"—but not really necessary to fulfill your apparent job description. As an antidote, I'd like to suggest that God was looking for someone to love the teens in your entire region (not just your church), so He put you in this particular place. Maybe He just used your pastor and his invitation to start you working with these kids ... to get your heart in the right position to reach all the others.

Now that God has you where He wants you, He can give you His vision for the teens of your region. You can be sure it will go perfectly in line with your pastor's vision for the local church. In other words, we must become vision driven and not just activity driven. We can do activities until we have worn ourselves out and still not reach many kids—and not fulfill our destiny.

As we approach the Lord about this vision for the youth in our area, we start by being convinced that "God wants all the young people in my region to come to Himself." This naturally leads to a mentality that we are going to take back this generation, whatever it costs. It is understanding that we are at war. It is refusing to let the enemy get away with murder any longer. It means "No more Mr. Nice Guy." Since this is serious, life-or-death work, we're going to roll up our sleeves, get our hands dirty, work hard, work smart, and capture the hearts of teens in our region.

Can you see how this philosophy is distinctly different from a goal of "just hanging out with the kids and loving them"? We cannot settle for a false sense of well-being by thinking, "The few that we have reached—we have loved them a lot and reached them in a quality way."

You were born for this moment. God needed a general to lead the armies of love that would enlist in fighting for this generation. He found you. Can you hear the marching band playing? *This is your moment.* Can you see the big picture? You have joined the ranks of other youth specialists all over the country who are taking their generalships seriously, determined to fully engage in this war.

WHAT DO YOU SEE, GENERAL?

The leader God desires is the one who can see where God wants to take the ministry. After talking and praying with your senior pastor about what your youth ministry should look like, your real work as a general begins: Asking the big questions. (And forget about how much you are already doing. Begin to dream a little.) A great place to start is to ask yourself this:

"If Jesus came back and took the job as youth pastor in my church, what would the ministry look like at the end of one year?"

I WANT TO end my life and I also am having a really hard time with my faith. I don't want to go to church anymore because my dad has stopped going and it feels like I am being tugged back and forth, between wanting to be with my dad and going to church. I am also questioning who Christ really is and if he even exists even though i have been raised in church all my life. Please keep me in prayer. *—Sarah*

How big would the group be? What would the worship look like? What about the training of teen leaders? How about the outreach and mission teams? What kind of "personality" would the group have? Start writing it all down. Your answers will bring you very close to Christ's vision for your ministry. After all, we are His hands and His feet here on earth to act in His place and represent Him.

"Wait a minute, Ron. You asked how many would be in the group. I don't think about numbers; I just concentrate on quality." Some of you just thought that. But why do we think we must chose between quality and quantity? Jesus wanted both.

> *Jesus came to them and said, "All authority in heaven and on earth has been given to me. Therefore go and make disciples of all nations, baptizing them in the name of the Father and of the Son and of the Holy Spirit, and teaching them to obey everything I have commanded you. And surely I am with you always, to the very end of the age. —Matthew 28:18-20*

Notice that He said to reach all nations (quantity) and to make them disciples (quality). We can have both. We must have both.

I am not talking about numbers here. I am talking about *people*. When you start reaching more, they just add up. You can't help it. Jesus loves every one of them, so let's start dreaming as big as He does—and let Him do the math.

As you dream and plan, keep a few important Do's and Don'ts in mind ...

- *DO* let vision generate provision. Some youth pastors become frustrated dreaming like this. They often think about the lack of funds. "I could do so much more if I just had the budget, but my church won't give me any money." They hide behind this excuse, and it actually paralyzes their ability to dream. The order is wrong. We must have the vision first, and then the provision will come. People will want to give to something that is actually going somewhere. If you get the money before the vision, you will squander it. You would end up using it on wasteful projects that don't take the big picture into consideration.

- *DO* reprioritize regularly. Some will look at the notion of developing a vision like this and ... sweat. They are already overworked and underpaid (or never paid). When they think of reaching more teens, it simply means they'll have to pedal even faster, until they die. They know the stress already bearing down on their family life; they can't imagine taking any more time away from home or job.

  The general realizes, though, that he must figure out how to reprioritize his life to accomplish the God-given objectives. If God is truly giving the vision for your local youth ministry, He surely has a way for you to achieve it and keep your family a priority. You certainly cannot accomplish the dream by doing more of what you are already doing, or the dream would have already come to pass.

- **DO** become a master delegator. As you develop this vision, it will surely demand at least two things. First, you will have to grow in your leadership ability. Reading books and gathering other leaders to mentor you in leading a larger ministry organization will be essential. Your pastor and other business leaders in your church would make excellent role models for you. It will also require thinking through all the roles that must be filled by others. I am talking about the grandmothers, grandfathers, businessmen, moms and dads, and college-age people you must have at the ready. If you really are the general, then you'll need to assign the troops their roles.

   Of course, before delegating, you may even need to recruit troops. And know this: You will never find all you need by hoping they'll just start hanging around the youth ministry looking for something to do. Most potential volunteers are looking for a leader worthy of their sacrifice. If they know that you have put in the time to leverage the sweat they put in, so that it is all a part of an overarching plan to make a great impact, then you will have a hard time keeping them away.

- **DON'T** just settle for activity. Clearly, we cannot settle for just finding things for the kids to do each Wednesday night. This is a great temptation because so much has been published in the name of youth ministry with the goal of "keeping them busy," one way or another. We can keep ourselves and our teens very busy with lots of good activities and curriculum. Yet in all our busyness, we'll never reach the potential God sees for our youth ministry.

- **DON'T** compete with First Church. Never compare and compete with the youth group down the street. The devil's youth group is still bigger than all the rest of ours put together. Let's look at the big picture. If all the generals in any given city got God's heart for the teens there, then we would end up covering all the bases. You will be attracted to, and anointed to reach, a particular type of teen that the youth pastor down the street may not be able to reach. Work together to win them.

ARE YOU READY TO TAKE THE INITIATIVE?

"Ron, I came here a year ago with no youth budget, no salary for me as a youth leader, with 120 people in our small-town church and only five kids in our youth group. This weekend we came back to Acquire the Fire and we still have no youth budget, no salary for me, and 120 people in our church. But we have 125 teens coming to youth group every week."

"Wow!" I said to the excited youth worker who had attended our Acquire the Fire conference a year earlier. "How did you do that?" I asked. He elaborated, "I just went home and did the things you taught us to do last year—and it worked!" I had taught them about beginning with vision and then gave them the tools to really develop the dream into reality.

One of those tools, for example, is my next book, titled *Revolution YM: The Official Field Manual for High-Impact Youth Ministry.* It will combine my teaching on vision, strategy, spiritual life, and more—everything youth workers need to catch God's vision for their ministries and run with it! Just call Cook Communications Ministries at 1-800-323-7543 and ask for product number 104507.

This is not a pipe dream. This is not pie in the sky. God is waiting for generals to take the initiative, dream His dreams, and then enlist the troops in the dream He gives them. Teens are waiting to be reached on the other side of that dream. If we don't dream, they may never be reached.

History will record the legacy of those of us involved in youth ministry today. Those who come after us will know that we were given a very special moment in time. And they will see whether or not we were faithful stewards of the leadership responsibilities God trusted us to fulfill. Let us be a generation of generals whom God found ready. Let us be faithful with the moment He's given us.

CHAPTER NINE

who are our sons and daughters?

"I'm so busy trying to raise my own kids! How on earth do you expect me to be involved with other people's kids?"

Did I just read your mind? While it's challenging enough to parent our offspring (I have two teens of my own), we must reckon with a chilling truth: If all of us who love God only reach our own teens, we will *lose a generation*. There simply aren't enough parents looking out for their teens' mental, emotional, and spiritual well being.

Joel 2:28 is often quoted by those excited about what God is going to do with a new generation. It speaks of the Spirit being poured out on "your sons and daughters." But who, exactly, are your sons and daughters?

Are they only the children growing up in your own household? Or might God expect us to take some responsibility, as well, for the

I AM 14 years old and I have just been saved and believe in God for a short time. pray for me that I wont fall into temptation and other things that are wrong from my past. pray that my peers will stop teasing me about my believing God because I want to show them what God has done for me and I don't want them to go to hell. it is just hard to get my point across to some of my friends who are not Christian because they say things to hurt me. I just want to help them so that God can be their provider. And also can you pray that you will help my parents to be able to go to church with me and help me to be brave enough to in a way preach to them. Thank you and God Bless. —*Jasmine*

other young ones growing up in the society we have created? In previous chapters we've seen the frightening picture of this young generation and the work of its determined destroyers. These are *our sons and daughters*. They are growing up in a world we have allowed to take shape. They are the sons and daughters of America. Ladies and gentlemen, I present your sons and your daughters.

They are not someone else's responsibility. Reaching out to them is more than an optional "kind gesture;" it is our duty. This is what we owe our children and the entire generation they will grow old with. These are the offspring that we, as a nation, are producing. These are the ones we are giving to the world to shape, in turn, their own future generations. Are we willing to mentor them?

MTV is more than willing. Hollywood is eager. Video gamers, rappers, and pornographers are lining up for the job. The drug dealers and gang bangers remain at the ready to take them. But what a tragedy when a teen walks right past a Bible-believing church member to get to one of these cultural death-dealers. The Christians were too preoccupied to notice.

EQUIPPING OUR OWN CHILDREN

But let's go ahead and start with the ones who actually have our own DNA. The Bible is clear that we must focus on these first if we are to qualify for ministry to others (see 1 Timothy 3:1-12). But suddenly we face a stark revelation: We can no longer parent the way we were parented. This is a new day.

Yes, sin is the same as it was when we were kids. But how dedicated and equipped—with the latest advertising and marketing methods—are the ones dishing it out to our young people! Perversion has sunk to an all-time low, on the order of Sodom and Gomorrah. Practicing effective parenting in this environment calls for drastic measures just to counter the enemy offensive launched against our children.

Drastic Measure #1: Limit, monitor, or totally prohibit screen-viewing time. Lies are dished out every day from types of media that are addictive even to toddlers. Our propensity to use TV or videos to "baby-sit" the kids harms them more than we know. In my family, we refused to allow TV to shape our lives or theirs. As our kids grew older, and using the Internet and video games became age-appropriate activities, we set some clear boundaries.

we are their parents. everything that goes into them, we ought to know before it does.

We are their parents. Everything that goes into them, we ought to know before it does. One day they will have to make these decisions on their own. Until then, it is our responsibility to keep their eyes and ears clear of the fog that will paint a false picture of reality on their hearts and minds. We have to teach them to see through it by keeping them out of it until they are old enough to identify the confusion of the world. Then, someday, they'll be prepared to use their own wise discernment to make good choices.

Drastic Measure #2: Keep teen bedrooms media-free. Many well-meaning parents have come to me in utter disbelief asking, "How could my little girl end up pregnant? We raised her in church and always tried to teach her the right things." But did they realize who else was teaching—or how ubiquitous the enemy is? Maybe they didn't understand that when they agreed to allow the TV and computer into their teen's bedroom they were inviting disaster. They may not have heard all the curse words in the secular music they allowed their teen to listen to, not to mention the teen's day-and-night immersion in the horrible values coming from those musicians. The enemy came right into their home and kidnapped the heart and mind of their teen.

"Go to your room!" doesn't have the same impact on kids as it used to, as a Knowledge Networks/SRI study finds that a significant number of children have various media and entertainment devices in their bedrooms. Based on interviews with 245 children ages eight to seventeen, the firm found that the kids' domain is rife with media usage.

According to the study, 61 percent have a television in their room. More than half the kids surveyed (57 percent) said that all their Internet usage takes place in their rooms, and 61 percent of their parents establish rules restricting Web use. Comparatively, 69 percent of kids without a Net connection in their rooms have parental restrictions.

I HAVE BEEN PRAYING to

the Lord about my dad. He answered my prayers. my dad e-mailed and asked to see me on my birthday, he asked for the dates of some of my activities to come see. though his attitude has not changed toward me, he is now dating a girl that could be my sister and I asked him why and he didn't seem to care how I felt about it. But I know that the Lord is still working in my life. The school thing has started to get better, but the boys pretty much grab me then hit my butt and I have no control. I wish I was at my old school, but i really want this to work. I once came to an Acquire the Fire and it really changed my life, I had accepted God in my life, but never really communicated with him. I now go to youth group regularly and now the president of the meet and greet team. My youth group leaders are really supportive and I can tell them almost anything. I don't think I have enough strength to tell my parents things. my mom is easy to talk to, but I can't tell her this. This past summer I was at a friend's b-day party and we were playing truth or dare. I had gotten dared to french kiss a girl and I did (every one knew me as a big daredevil). well a girl that didn't like me made a rumor and said i was lesbian and i'm really not. Everyone at my school started calling me that and it was so depressing I felt like shooting myself although i never would. Since changing schools I've lost a lot of friendships. It is really sad one of my best friends and i made a promise at the end of sixth grade that we would never stop being best friends and now i wouldn't even really call us friends. It is so sad so would you e-mail me with any suggestions? — *Carie*

"Kids with own-room media access represent an important sub-group of media users," said David Tice, Knowledge Networks/SRI vice president, Client Service. "Their behavior is more self-directed, in terms of linking media with each other and with other activities, and they have less parental supervision."[1]

Supervision is the key! We, as parents, must commit to shaping our kids' characters by making sure we are aware of all media influence in their lives. We can't shut down MTV and Hollywood overnight, but we can shut down their control in our homes. We can protect our kids from the brainwashing the rest of their generation is receiving. I know it is tempting to let teens have cable TV in their room, but we must decide what kind of family we are going to be.

Drastic Measure #3: Make a firm family decision about "who we are." Here's the choice: Are we going to be a media-centered family or a relationship-centered family? If we choose what most of America is choosing (even Christians), we will be the former. We will run our lives by what shows up on the TV Guide.

There's a better way. My wife, Katie, and I have been hypersensitive to what our kids watched on TV from their earliest days. For many years we only had one TV in the house, and we seldom turned it on. Our kids watched, as small children, only approved programs for about one or two hours per week. They didn't get to know all the popular cartoons and other kid's programs. They knew nothing of the latest toys crammed down the throats of their peers, unless they saw them at stores. We would occupy ourselves with other games and activities. We'd try to enjoy each other rather than "veg out" with some form of media. (We did allow them to see videos, mostly Christian children's videos, but these were strictly monitored.) This may seem like a drastic lifestyle, but we do live in drastic times.

As we taught our kids from a young age about the so-called "value-free" influence of the world, we grew to trust them. Eventually, even if we weren't in the room with them, we knew they wouldn't choose to watch garbage. They would switch the channel if something bad came on. Yet, over the years, more and more perverse commercials would flash in front of their eyes while they were changing channels. This is where we drew the line. We began to never let them watch any TV unless we were right there with them.

If we start young, they won't know what they are missing; they'll learn to really enjoy time as family. Here's a little scenario from one family that seems to illustrate everything I've been saying:

When our two daughters were about eleven and twelve years old, they called a family meeting with a very important matter to discuss. After sitting down in the living room, they told us they had a proposal for us to consider. They had made banners and signs for this event and used a different one for each point they made. They wanted a trampoline for the back yard. They talked of all the advantages of having one: more time playing outside, more family fun, and less TV watching. That last point got our attention. They didn't really watch much TV anyway, but it excited us that they were willing to bargain even that away.

They told us they had done the research and knew how much a particular trampoline would cost; they were willing to pay for half of it. "So, what do you think of our deal?" they asked.

Carefully considering the opportunity before us, we made a counterproposal. We told them we would pay for all of the trampoline if they were willing to give up all TV during the coming year. They had to think long and hard about it; in fact, they wanted the rest of the evening to discuss it between them.

The next morning they told us that they kept going back and forth with all the pros and cons of each choice. Finally, they decided that the part of them that wanted to sit, zombie-like, in front of a television set couldn't compete with the part that longed for the engrossing thrill of flying through the air with reckless abandon. They took us up on our offer and had their trampoline within two days. They also kept their commitment, without a fight, for a solid year.

What a difference it made! Not only did we do a lot more things as a family, but the kids took up a regular lifestyle without TV. They never wondered what they were missing. Their normal life now revolved around many other things— but not media. Three years later, it is still like that.

HELPING OUR KIDS BECOME THE INFLUENCERS

After shielding and shaping our children's character, our real mandate begins. We must help them from a very young age not merely to be Christians, but to be potent Christians. When they walk into the room they should be the ones who shape the conversation. They must be the salt and the light that Jesus talked about. And it isn't just for the extroverts. This is a mandate; if teens learn to be ashamed of their faith (because of their parents' lifestyles), then they will think it rather strange that we want their friends to come to Christ.

Let's let them know they were born for greatness! They are here to make an impact. God brought them into the world because He has something special that only he or she can do. There is greatness inside them. Since my kids were babies, I've prayed over them: "Use them, Lord, to change the world and to impact every single person they meet."

In the minds of our children, it should not be "if" God wants to use them but "how" God wants to use them. As you pray over them and encourage them to discern how God wants to use them now (not just when they grow up), be ready to rally to their side in support. We need to teach them to dream God's dreams and then go after those dreams.

They may not know how to start, and that is where you will be of great help. They may have bigger dreams than yours, but don't let that intimidate you; it is a compliment to your parenting skill. You certainly don't want to pour cold water on their passionate, idealistic notions of how they could change their school or change their world. Just help them think through what it would take, in practical terms, to accomplish such feats. As your kids come to you with their ideas, you'll be joining the ranks of other parents throughout history whose children changed the world.

They may want to go on a mission trip to another country. Maybe you have never traveled outside of the country yourself—and it sounds like a lot of money. But don't say "No" too quickly. Or they may want to start a Christian band or a Bible club at school. Why should only the secular teens be the ones who are supported by their parents to start a band? I think with sadness about someone like Avril Lavigne, who got her big break at age 16, a huge secular music sensation. She is "changing her generation" with lyrics like: "I'm naked around you, and it feels so right" or "I don't give a d——."

we must help them from a very young age not merely to be Christians, but to be potent Christians.

If your kids aren't overflowing with ideas about how to change the world for God, try using a challenge that I've used with each of my own children, even from a very young age. I ask them: "How do you think the Lord wants to use you this year in school?" I ask them to pray about it, and I keep asking them until they have an answer. It may take days or even weeks. Then, when they come back with an idea, I get involved helping them accomplish the dream. Some of their ventures for God have included:

- *Writing a book (at age 9)*
- *Designing and programming a Web page for preteen girls (at age 13)*
- *Singing in front of thousands, and on television (age 12/13)*
- *Starting a Bible study at school*

Our kids need to know we believe in them and that it's just natural for them to be involved in changing the world and shaping their generation for the Kingdom. Most of them will never do it without our help.

FULLY ENGAGING YOUR TEEN'S GENERATION

Now that we have the correct focus on our teens at home, it's time for us to own up to our responsibility to reach their generation. We need to ask ourselves, "What kind of world do we want for them? What kind of world do we want our grandchildren to grow up in?" It is not enough to shape our offspring; we need to look at the macro picture. We must find our role in engaging the generation directly, not just through our kids.

"Where do I start?" you ask. "What would I even do?" The very least you can do is to fill your car with your teens' unchurched friends every week! We do it for soccer practice and cheerleading—why not for their souls? Let's go again to our survey for some practical answers. Listen to the kinds of things youth pastors are saying about parents of teens when asked some pointed questions. (First, the bad news.)

QUESTION:
"DO THE TEENS IN YOUR YOUTH GROUP HAVE INVOLVED PARENTS?"

- No. It's almost as if they just blindly hand over the lives of their teens to anybody who is willing to spend a Sunday evening with them.
- Some have gotten involved. The interesting trend is that "churched" parents, those who have grown up in the church, are less active than "unchurched" or parents of new believing students. So the answer is no, we do not have many parents that get involved.
- Parents usually are my biggest problem! They often seem to know better than me and always know what, exactly, I need to do for their kids to get them "on fire for the Lord." But if that's true, why don't they do these things at home so the kids can come to youth group on fire?
- No involvement whatsoever. It is so hard, because parents do not want to bring their teens to church, yet they wonder why our society is the way it is. Not only are parents not bringing their teens, but the teens are not bringing their friends because parents won't pick up their friends to bring them to church.
- Parental involvement is virtually non-existent in my youth ministry.

"Okay, I'm a parent. What things could I be doing?" First, talk with your youth pastor. Tell him or her you want to help. After he comes out of his coma (from the shock), ask him what you can do to serve the local youth ministry. Don't be distraught if she has to think

it really makes a difference in the lives of kids who often don't have parental involvement at home (if they live with their parents at all).

for few days before responding, since this has probably never happened before.

After you receive an assignment, you may feel you want to do even more. You can. There's no rule keeping you from joining "Moms in Touch" (**www.momsintouch.com**); always bringing other teens to church besides your own; conversing with teens in the lobby of the church before services—and a host of other ideas that caring parents have proven to be effective, as described by youth pastors:

QUESTION:
"WHEN PARENTS HAVE GOTTEN INVOLVED, WHAT KINDS OF THINGS HAVE THEY DONE?"

- They serve as sponsors or chaperones. At Acquire the Fire last spring we brought 65 students—and 23 parents came with us. We had a great time! Thirty-four parents participated in the parent seminar during the month beforehand. We chartered buses for both events, and the parents had a ball.
- I "require" parents to go on at least one trip to Mexico during the four years their student is in high school. It's been fun to watch them "watch" their student doing ministry. It has changed parents.

- They volunteer for almost everything. I had one mom say she would do all the secretarial work. Others just pray for us. One dad stepped up and did the fundraiser organizing. Parents go on outings with us and help drive. Most of all they feed the kids.

- I have two couples who are willing to do whatever it takes to reach kids. They open their house any time of day or night. Many of these teens feel that these are "second parents" to them.

- All of our youth leaders are parents, and I've seen them go on mission trips with these kids, serving side by side with them. They're great counselors for the small groups. They take teens to Christian concerts. Bottom line, they understand the importance of discipling teens through word and example.

- Simply having parents who take time to bring by a snack to our events or drive a car for transporting students to camp are huge things for our students to see. We remind the students all the time that the adults are very busy—but they care so greatly about the students that they will take time out of their day to help out in little ways.

- We have a few parents who really attach themselves to specific kids in the youth group, usually new members, in order to develop relationships and to mentor them spiritually. It really makes a difference in the lives of kids who often don't have parental involvement at home (if they live with their parents at all).

QUESTION:

"CAN YOU SHARE SOME STORIES ABOUT PARENTS WHO HAVE REALLY MADE A DIFFERENCE IN THE LIVES OF YOUR TEENS?"

- "Mrs. Smith" is part of another family that started coming to our church because her son and daughter came to youth group. She just became a sponsor last month, but really, she had become a sponsor even before I gave her a Job Description. She would have at least ten teens over to her house every night. Some of the youth with major problems have found a mother in her. It was only natural that she come and work with the team. It is not uncommon to hear the youth calling out for "Mom"—when they are looking for Mrs. Smith.

- We have a grandmother of three who goes beyond the call of duty. She is not only raising the three kids on a very low income, but she goes out and brings other teenagers into her home as well. Nearly all have come to Christ and the parents are now coming to church because of her devotion to these teens. She will sometimes make up to four trips in her truck to pick these kids up for church on Sundays.

- In our mother/daughter Bible study, it was really awesome. A lot of bonding occurred between families, and the moms were really willing to speak up and ask questions that I know the girls were probably curious about (but not open enough to ask). The mothers got a chance to see the spiritual maturity of their daughters through this study as well. We also had a women's Bible study that invited the girls of the congregation to come join them for a month. The girls would ask the women to tell what they know about God, marriage, kids, education, and life—things they wish they had known as a teen. It really had an impact on my girls, with all these moms being honest with them about their struggles and triumphs. It was great.

- A couple of our parents have been instrumental in getting young people on the mission field. These parents have without fail given every young person at least $100 each time they have gone on mission trips. When there is an event, they ask me whether any of the students need funds to attend. They sometimes will ask a student to do some labor to get the money, in order to teach them a work ethic, but they always give what they can. Even in financially hard times, they have given. This shows to the young people how much they believe in them. Many of the young people have told me that even when they wanted to quit, because so-and-so gave them money, they pressed on, not wanting to disappoint these parents.

KNOWING THE TIME IS SHORT

Look into the faces of the next ten teens you meet. Imagine that eight of them will enter a Christless eternity. Which eight will you choose? There is time to reach all of them—but a limited time. And all the while, things seem to be getting worse for so many young people. I came across an online news article recently that shook me to the core. It was a story from San Diego telling about how popular it is these days for pimps to go to junior high schools and malls looking to fill a fast-growing network of underage prostitution rings.

The young teens, who are promised significant rewards, eventually drop out of school and begin making the rounds from city to city, offering their bodies for pay. These young people aren't necessarily from poverty-stricken families, either. Many of the 14 and 15 year olds hail from affluent neighborhoods.

One of the girls, 17-year-old Torrey Flake, had disappeared for nine weeks, with her mother assuming she'd simply run away. But authorities suspect she was grabbed by a prostitution ring and may have been taken to Mexico, enslaved there in a life of horrible deprivation and abuse.

San Diego police, trying to stem the tide of childhood prostitution, often feel as if they're fighting a losing battle. And here's why, in the closing words of the article: Police say "the key isn't so much policing as it is parenting."[2]

Parenting is crucial in this battle for our young people. We have a short window of time; they are only young once. Let us be the parents who seize the moment. Let's be the ones who take responsibility for the sons and daughters of America. May we be willing to sacrifice our time, our personal convenience, our best energies to keep from sacrificing a whole generation.

1 "Kids Are Media Users Too," by Robyn Greenspan, October 9, 2003, on **www.clickz.com**.

2 "Teen Prostitution on Rise in California," Thursday, January 27, 2005. Article on the Web at **http://www.foxnews.com/story/0,2933,145493,00.html**.

CHAPTER TEN

everyone has a role in this rescue!

Each of us knows young people who've been affected by the battle described in this book. The good news is that there are caring adults in America like you who can jump into the middle of the fray and rescue them. We can see an entire generation change directions. But we need to take hold of the steering wheel and help them veer away from the edge of the cliff. To put it another way: If every caring adult in the land rallied around the youth in their communities, then we would see a miracle in this country.

"But what use am I? What difference can one person make?" Did you just think that? Carefully read through this chapter and see exactly what difference you can make. I'm going to rely heavily on the survey reports of youth pastors to tell you in their own words what they need. Surely you will find the perfect place to fit in, whether you

as men, we are the ones in society tasked with protecting the next generation. we must protect them!

are a business person, a senior citizen, or a young adult. Some of the ideas will apply directly to you, others will assist people you know. Read each section so you'll understand the overall plan that you can take back to the teens in your community.

LET THE WARRIORS ARISE:
THE ROLE OF MEN

We have heard for so long that there is a problem with this generation of young people. So women, especially moms, have begun reaching out. But the question is: Where are the men and fathers?

Where are the warriors who filled stadiums just a few years ago, promising to build strong families? Where are the men who stood in groups of fifty thousand strong cheering for Jesus? Where are the 1.2 million who went to the mall in Washington D.C. to make promises to God? Where are they when our kids need them the most?

It is time for us to rise up like an angry father who has just realized his kids have been kidnapped, robbed, brainwashed, and tortured—all in the name of entertainment. Any father would growl with anger and determination to rescue his beloved young one. Any man worth the name would gladly go out of his way and take great risks to bring a child like this to safety.

Well men, young victims are all around us. We must step up to the plate and do something. It is not our youth pastor's job. As men, we are the ones in society tasked with protecting the next generation. We must protect them!

Everyone must get involved, especially the protectors of the home. If you say "I don't have time," we lose. If you say "I don't relate very well to teens," we lose. If you say "I can't give money right now," we lose. We lose our posterity. We lose what America stands for. We lose the wholesome world our kids and grandkids deserve to grow up in. We lose a generation.

Why are we men so important in this battle? It has to do with our leadership influence, our ability to sacrifice and protect, and our connection to money-making.

We have the influence. Men have a weighty influence in the home and community. We often use our masculine gravitas to "negotiate another deal," and we can also use it on behalf of teens being pillaged by media money-mongers. The entertainment industry moguls and their minions will do anything, sell anything, put anything on a video screen, just to make a buck. And they are very good at what they do.

I HAVEN'T been to church in over 5 years and basically just wasn't with Jesus. I wasted a lot of time and don't really have anything good to show for my life. I've been trying to read the Bible everyday and talk to God. I'm gonna try to start going back to the church I used to go to when I was in high school and youth group. Only thing is I'm not sure how to go about it. I don't want to just show up and be like here I am. So I guess I'm trying to figure out how to go back. Plus I've never been the kind of person to just go up to people I've never talked to and just start talking to them so I'm kind of hesitant about going back. —*Adam*

Someone—a man—must stand in their way.

We must make a loud noise, and make it for a long time. We must make that noise in our community and in our nation. How? By giving our time, our money, our influence. We can take teens to church with us, take them to youth ministry meetings, even if they live far out of our way. We must go to retreats with these kids, take them to huge events where they can see they are not alone in trying to serve God. We must show them that they are more important to a generation of men than career advancement at all costs.

Imagine broadening your influence and pulling your town's businessmen together to discuss involvement in the war. This is a time of action. You may have never done this before, but exceptional times call for exceptional responses. Desperate times call for desperate actions.

I can hear some of you backing away already. "I don't really feel led to do something like that; it would take so much of my time and energy." Just put a bullet in your pocket, and touch it every time you get those feelings—you'll *feel lead!*" And if you don't feel like a "man of influence" in your community, now is the time to become one. You will exert influence when you know something is so important you just cannot keep silent. The battle cry for a generation is that important.

We know how to sacrifice. We know how to gut it out at "crunch time." But what message do we send when young people see us working until midnight every night, taking trips out of town, making enormous personal sacrifices for the sake of our careers while telling them that we're too busy to pull them from the burning car? There are young ones all around us brutalized by this raging war, and we walk by, too busy to help. We move to the other side of the road with our cell phone to our ear, pretending not to notice. We walk around the teen in the ditch—sort of like the priest and the Levite in the parable of the Good Samaritan.

But we need to be the Samaritan.

We are willing to sacrifice for our job, but not for a bleeding group of teens programmed for destruction by the media? Is that the men we want to be? Is that the legacy we want to extend to future generations? If the answer is "no," then we'll give some of our weekends, some of our convenience, some of our discretionary time. We'll give, and lives will be changed forever.

Think of the sacrifices being made right now by the enemy. While you sit and read this paragraph, there are literally thousands of people working non-stop to pump garbage into the teens in your town. They are writing and producing foul-mouthed songs that your kids will soon be memorizing. They are working all-nighters right now to degrade teen morality. People are working their way up the ladder at various networks, thinking of new ways to make teen programming more racy, to keep the ratings up and to keep the revenues up. Others are programming Web pages as you sit comfortably reading this, pages designed to imprint our kids' brains in ways that could destroy their marriages and family lives, long into the next generation. If they can sacrifice to make a name and a buck for themselves, how can we not give and fight for a much greater cause? Let it never be said that we lost a generation because we were not willing to sacrifice as much as the destroyers of youth culture. No, not on our watch.

We're in business—and have the finances. Don't skip this part just because you know you may feel convicted to give. I can hear you thinking, "You had to bring up money, didn't you?"

> let it never be said that we lost a generation because we were not willing to sacrifice as much as the destroyers of youth culture.

But who is going to finance this war? Everyone knows it costs a lot of money to wage war. Who is willing to invest? Who thinks teens are important enough? Is MTV's ambition for money more powerful than our desire to protect young souls?

There are youth pastors with dreams in your area. They want to reach out in a massive way to the hurting teens in your region. They want to build youth ministry centers. They need busses and vans to pick up the kids. They need sound and light equipment so their Gospel presentations will be second to none. Tracts need to be printed, videos edited, and lots of food purchased to create an environment where kids are opening their hearts to loving youth workers. What a heart-breaking reality: hundreds of youth workers all over this land pray to God with a compelling vision to reach the teens in their communities …with no idea how to fund it all. We see the bad news about some young people on TV and think, "What can I possibly do about it?"

Passionate workers all over America know exactly what to do. They know how to reach teens right where they are. They know the keys to touching their hearts. They have been doing it for little or no pay for years, perfecting the craft. The only thing that lies between them and influencing a huge amount of teens in a positive way is: that green stuff in your wallet. What a tragedy to think that so many could actually be helped and rescued, if only a few good men would say yes to an eternal investment. What a shame to amass a huge nest egg while we lose a generation. How embarrassed will we be to know that if we would all have invested in this generation, while the window was open (now), we could have avoided disaster.

It can be fun. Make as much money as you can, and give it to the sources that can make the biggest impact. Think about how mad you would make the devil. Seizing the American dream of making lots of money, and using that very money to perpetuate an America that honors God above money? This is the lifestyle of a man who will die happy.

I recently met with a businessman regarding a fundraising project. I told him of our $30 million goal and asked if he would consider giving $1 million over the next three years. I had explained to him the vision and strategy, told him why we thought it would make a lasting impact on youth. (I really went to share the vision, not just to ask for money.)

After I asked, he paused for about four seconds and then said, "Okay, I'll do that, but on one condition." I became a little anxious at this point, not knowing what he would ask. "I want you to pray for my business ventures. Pray for my companies, that all the business deals go right, and that God blesses. As soon as He blesses the company, I will pay my commitment." You can be sure I was regularly pleading to God on his behalf. Only six weeks later, he called to tell me the good news and wanted me to come by so he could give me the first third of his million-dollar commitment. I like that kind of business partner.

Could you find someone to partner with? Ask him or her to pray like crazy for God to bless you and your business—so you can give it away. Think of the fervent prayers you will get. Think of how much fun you'll have making business deals with souls in the balance. There is a reason God gave you the ability to make money; discover that reason, and you discover a piece of your Kingdom assignment.

There are so many different and creative ways you can be involved as a man of influence and/or business owner. When asked, youth pastors had much to say about such men and women. Just look at what your own peers have done to stand by those who labor full time for teens caught in the crossfire:

QUESTION:

"WHAT HAVE BUSINESSMEN DONE TO ASSIST WITH YOUR YOUTH MINISTRY?"

- We have a local business that gives $100 per month to our ministry. We also have two doctors (whose daughters come to youth group) who live in two different cities outside of our area. They've given close to $24,000 during the past year.

- We once needed some assistance with bills from an event where we rented a bus, and the church treasurer was concerned about us spending too much. My pastor sought out the local funeral director and was able to get that awesome guy to bless us with $1,000 for the bus for the weekend! That man has since told me that if we ever need help again, that I am to go ahead and ask him.

- We have an owner of a restaurant in our town who donates food or supplies anytime we need them. We also have a surveyor who donates his time and office so we can go on the Internet to check out upcoming events. He gives us any office supplies we might need.

- The local Dominos is owned by one of our parents. We get discounts, freebies, and now even a climbing wall that's available to us for free. A great addition to our activities!

- One of our businessmen owns a condo up north. He lets us use it for our leadership retreats.

- One business leader went out and bought us a six-foot dual BBQ pit, so we can do cookouts with our outreach program. We also have a businessman who owns a shoe warehouse. He offers our youth group excellent discounts and has become the "sole" provider of gym shoes for our church.

- I wanted to put on a Daddy/Daughter Date Night and I asked a few of the businesswomen of the congregation to help out. One owns a printing business, one is currently an advertising agent but used to work as a party planner, and another works for the city but has skill as a decorator. I put this whole event in these women's hands. It was a great success with gorgeous invitations, amazing decorations, wonderful music. And it cost $3 a person because most everything was donated.

BEING THERE: THE ROLE OF SENIORS

"Ron, what can a grandmother do to help these kids today?"

These were the words of desperation uttered by "Memaw," my wife's precious, 84-year-old grandmother. She wanted to help but had no idea of the role she could play.

She's like many senior citizens who have worked hard throughout their lives for the rich reward of a more comfortable retirement. But many are feeling that, although its fun to play and travel to their hearts' content, they want to feel more useful.

If you are arriving at this stage in life, you have many advantages when it comes to helping the younger generation. First, you probably have more discretionary time than anyone else in society. Were your free time to be strategically deployed in this battle for the soul of a generation, what an amazing impact you could have! Instead of doing so many things that just "occupy," you could get involved in changing young lives for the Lord.

Because of the breakup of the American family, teens today are far less connected to any extended family. Many don't even know their grandparents (or have a distant relationship, at best). All your warm memories of spending time at Grandpa's house are simply absent from their memory banks. So, think about filling in, becoming the grandparents for this generation and not simply for your own grandchildren. What an amazing role God has for you to play with a very isolated generation of teens. What a legacy!

In such a role, you will pass along your wisdom, moral integrity, and personal character. We can already see who is shaping them in the opposite directions. But what if a massive army of seniors rose up to take responsibility for changing that direction? You have so much wisdom to impart. Our young people today desperately need mentors to pass on to them what many of their parents either didn't have or didn't take the time to share.

It would be easy to think, "Wait a minute; I did my work in life, I've already raised my kids." While this may be true, for some reason your kids' generation has not been able to stand against the formidable odds of the modern techno-terrorists. As I have said, this is not longer fair. It is no longer the "same challenges" all teens of the past have dealt with. We are facing a new kind of reality, a full-blown assault. And it is going to take every hand on deck to launch an effective counterattack.

"But I wouldn't know what to say to them. They look so different!" Yet it's amazing how normal they begin to appear when you stop to listen to them. Just get to know one or two teens in your church. No matter what they look like on the outside, they really are overgrown children within a body that is usually larger than the maturity inside. Most often their clothes and "jewelry" simply express a desire to fit in with peers who look the same. But really they are soft inside.

I remember walking around the concourse of an arena packed with ten thousand teenagers during a break at one of our Acquire the Fire conferences. Everyone sort of looked the same—until I saw this one young lady with bright red hair and dressed all in black leather. Everything on her head seemed to be pierced, including her tongue. I grabbed her hand to shake it and said, "Your hair looks ... awesome!"

She replied, "It does?"

I repeated myself, "Your hair looks awesome!"

Then she said (the best she could, with a steel bar through her tongue): "Do you know where I can find information about these mission trips?"

As if to say, "Do you think even someone like me could change the world?"

Wow. My heart was moved, and I am so glad I did not judge that book by its cover.

Just read on to discover what seniors have done to reach out to teens. They have found all kinds of creative ways to express their gifts and make a lasting impact on teens in their communities.

QUESTION:
"IN WHAT PRACTICAL WAYS HAVE SENIORS GOTTEN INVOLVED WITH YOUR YOUNG PEOPLE?"

Just loving them

- One senior couple works the kitchen for all of our events, even though their kids are grown. They are "adopting" all of the kids, and are willing to bake cookies and serve snacks, even though they live 45 minutes away and don't get home until after 1:00 A.M.
- We have a 78-year-old lady who is God's gift to our youth. She does exactly what we all should do: She just loves them. And they know it. She brings in little homemade treats from time to time (usually just after the first of the month) and the kids love it. If the

our young people today desperately need mentors to pass on to them what many of their parents either didn't have or didn't take the time to share.

rest of the congregation, especially the leaders and decision-makers, would love the youth as she does, we could really make a difference for the Kingdom.

- "Grandma Shirley" has helped in the youth ministry for years. We have a cafe, and she helps run it for two Wednesdays a month. All the kids love being around her and she loves coming every week. She rocks to our music, and finds little articles about our favorite bands and clips them for us. She is truly a blessing!

- Our church has a great seniors group called "Jubilees." They love getting together with the youth, and the youth love them, too. I remember after one "Youth Sunday" one of the eldest Jubilees tearfully told the youth that it was the best service she had ever sat through. When our youth group rapidly began expanding, one of the Jubilees bought us a minibus at a school district auction.

Praying for them.

- Several of our seniors pray for the teens regularly. Some also sponsor students if the kids do not have funds available for events. I am pursuing a concept that will try to join these two groups through a mentoring/prayer venture. My desire is for every teen to have a "seasoned saint" praying and meeting with him or her.

- The largest way our elderly people get involved is through prayer partners. Each year we set out information and pictures of each student and they choose one to pray for and encourage throughout the year. They send cards, gifts, and goodies on special occasions. It is good for both sides to gain understanding of one another and realize what God can do at all seasons of life.

- I found the praying matriarchs and patriarchs of the church and asked them each to take on a high school student to mentor/prayer partner with. It took a lot of coaxing, but it eventually happened—and it is awesome! The seniors have really begun to talk to the kids, and the kids now are starting to approach the seniors on their own. The kids sometimes go to different seniors to help them out with different problems they have been having. There has been a whole new level of respect for the teens and a new level of freedom of fellowship between the two groups.

Showing hospitality

- Some of our seniors make snacks and goodies for our events. They are behind the scenes but we make sure our teens know about their kindness.
- I have a senior who always asks what she can do to help. She fixes a meal every month and supports us with her prayers and finances. She is 70+.
- One grandmother has been our cook on trips and is dearly loved for her cinnamon rolls—and for her big heart!
- One very elderly lady in our church invited the students to her home a couple of times a year for encouragement, food, and fun. She couldn't do a lot, but she let them know that she prayed for them regularly. She would hug them and always speak to them at church. She would go out of her way to spend just a few moments with each young person every Sunday. She knew all their names. Every young person attended her funeral and even though they couldn't really pinpoint all the things she did for them, they knew she loved them and that they had lost a friend.

Being generous

- Our seniors sponsor teens in the youth ministry through a fund we call the Impact Fund. It's like anyone would normally sponsor a kid through World Vision, etc.
- We have a pair of grandparents who really help financially—and with verbal encouragement.

don't wait to be invited. history itself is inviting you to jump into the fray.

- Seniors helped us with a fundraiser. They said it was the most fun they had ever had—and they didn't realize how great the youth really are.
- We created the "Sweetie Pie Club"—a group of elderly women charged with overseeing a fundraiser for the teens. They take orders for Easter pies and make the pies themselves. Both the Elders and the teens have a wonderful time with the event.
- One senior lady in our church has really reached out to the youth. She has come in and talked to them about relationship evangelism. She has been taking them through Scripture and teaching them the Romans road. She also has invested about $10,000 in our youth ministry for tracts, missions, conferences, and Scripture memory cards. She's amazing.

Mentoring them

- One of the deacons is a widowed woman with a big heart and a lot of energy. She often stopped by the youth meeting to see whether there was anything the youth needed, or anything she could help with. One evening she overheard a few of the youth talking about their grades and their distress about barely passing. She approached me and offered to help tutor at the church in the evenings. Turns out, this woman—who is older than my grand-mother—is a whiz at not only Algebra, but Trig, Geometry, and Calculus as well! Who knew?!
- Being a parent, I have had my daughter come home telling of the senior adults in our church coming into class to share their

I WAS thirteen when my unknown quest for God began. My father died, my mother snapped and my life went downhill. My mother got with a guy that drank from sun up till sun down. He found joy in slapping me around. He would choke me, kick me, stomp me. Not only that, he verbally abused me. So did my mom. A few months into their relationship, he shoved me on a couch and tried to rape me. I'm a male and I'm still scarred over this. Soon after that, he left and my mother found another man. He was black, but that didn't bother me. He was kind. Then he introduced me to drugs. I started drugs, sex, anything to fill a void of love I'd been missing. Not long after him, I moved in with my grandmother. There, I became depressed, tried to end my life. Each time I put a blade to my skin, I felt something tug on my heart and I'd drop the blade, drop to my knees and cry. This went on for several months until one night a friend, who I call "Mom," took me to a youth lock-in. I'd been going to church, but just for girls and to sleep. However, that night, during the singing they had an altar call. My legs began to move, I started to shake. Slowly I got up and made my way to the altar. There, glimpses of everything I'd been through passed before my eyes. After the visions had faded I saw a face with a beard and long hair with a crown of thorns. His mouth opened and the words "I love you" came from him. I dropped to my knees, tears rolling down my face like never before and called out to Jesus saying, "Fill me! Take these scars and the pain away and fill me." It was that night I accepted Jesus Christ into my heart and changed my life. The next day, I trashed all my secular items, like pornography, violent CDs, and other evil things. I now go to church every time the doors are open. I help other teens like me, I even lead a youth service every month where I give a sermon. True, my journey to Jesus started out like a trip to hell, but now I know where I'm going. Straight to heaven! —*Brice (15)* stories. Dating experiences, coming to Christ—they have real-life stories. She still remembers them, and I really think it puts a whole new spin on life for them. We even have some seniors who have "adopted" the teens and made them feel loved. One elderly man in our church has pretty much lost his sight, but his heart size makes up for it. He never lets a moment pass to tell the teen girls that he and his wife pray for them daily. Others are willing to help with homework. It's great.

Compare all these amazing stories to the heartbreaking responses from youth pastors who were asked the following question:

QUESTION:
"HAVE ANY ELDERLY PEOPLE GOTTEN INVOLVED IN YOUR CHURCH'S YOUTH MINISTRY?"

- Not really, except for supporting us financially through fundraisers. Oh, well, I do have one lady who discreetly slips me a twenty every couple of months to use however I need and I use it for pop, snacks, etc.
- No, our church is mostly elderly and they choose not to be involved other than to occasionally give or spend a bit of money when we do a fundraiser. They are not very accepting or welcoming to the kids.
- No. The only criticism I have of our youth ministry is that the elderly seem disconnected from the teens. Our society has changed to the point that many elderly members don't understand today's youth and the issues they face.

As you can see, there are many opportunities for seniors to reach out to teens in practical ways. At this critical time in our nation's history, teens and youth pastors are crying out for adults to get involved in the lives of these young ones. Will you find your assignment among this new generation? Don't wait to be invited. History itself is inviting you to jump into the fray.

SHOW THE WAY:
THE ROLE OF TWENTY-SOMETHINGS

Maybe you've just left your teenage years behind. But you certainly remember wanting to see a vivid example of living Christianity. So many teens cannot imagine what it would actually look like to enter into their adult lives thriving in their faith and still being a relatable person. Can you hear the heart of this teen:

> *"If it wasn't for the twenty-somethings, none of us youth would be the Christians that we are—and most of us would not be Christians at all. They have taken time, over and over, just to do things for us personally. Last summer, our youth leaders spent hundreds of dollars as well as hours on trying to raise money for a group to go on a mission trip when they couldn't even go. And when there was money left over, they continued to put it toward the youth group. They are such a blessing.*

Can you sense the significance of the example she observed?

If you are in your college years, the potency of your example cannot be underestimated. You have enormous impact on lives just a few years your junior. Teens constantly look to the "little bit older" person for their cues in life, good or bad. Those who are 11 or 12 look to the 15 and 16 year olds. Those who are 16 and 17 look to 19 and 20 year olds to see where they could be. If you are in your early twenties,

what if you went beyond just making a living and determined to make a difference?

then you are actually a part of this massive group of "Millennials." You are a forerunner for them. They are looking at you, and you are called to lead the way. What they see in you is what they will become. You have the chance to set the pace for the largest generation in America since the Boomers. Where they go, so will go America. So will go the world.

In the midst of preparing for your career, don't forget the role you play for this generation, whether you like it or not. For some reason God saw fit to put you on the leading edge, so it's time to seize the day. If you have moved away to college, great. Do what I did in college and find a youth ministry somewhere to plug into and serve. Every youth minister in the world is hungry to have older examples for his teens.

You will not be young forever, so use the influence you have to impact them while you can. If you think you are not called to "youth ministry," think again. Your position in life, and the timing of your birth, puts you in command of where they will go. You can try to avoid this responsibility and pretend it isn't so. But teens will pay the price.

Youth leaders from all over the country have commented on the imperative role that young adults play in their ministries. Just look at their comments and notice how important the young adults have been. Their examples give us a cue as to the kinds of roles you can play in this battle for the soul of a generation.

Be the example

- Robby is in his early twenties, a U.S. marine. He has been a great role model for our youth. They have someone who's following Christ and working and living in the world with everyday challenges, trying to do the right thing. He loves spending time with them encouraging them to stay on the right track. He shows them they can have fun and still be a Christian.

- One of our young adults told me: "I have been able to talk in depth with our girls about the importance of purity in their relationships. I have made my share of mistakes and am open with them about the pain and consequences I've gone through because I didn't stick to my purity commitment. The girls feel more comfortable talking to me because they know I understand the pressures of today. Being 22, I'm world smart about what is going on today, and am not afraid to talk about it with them. This is a huge example to the students who feel that they have to be older to do anything of value. They are seeing students in leadership as well."

Be the mentor

- One of my leaders saw a young man who was really struggling in middle school. He began to take him everywhere with him—to soccer games, the gym, to his family's home. As the leader showed the student how to live with Christ every day, there was a dramatic change in the student. He came to know Christ in a personal way, made some positive life changes, and has since become one of the student leaders in the youth ministry.

- My teens ask for these twenty-something leaders by name. They want to spend time with them because they realize that these people want to spend time with teens. One of my strongest youth leaders saw a need for some unity within our teen group.
- One guy is a youngish married guy without kids who talks to any of the guys who want to about sexuality. He meets with them in small groups or one-on-one and answers any of their questions. He challenges them to be pure and encourages them to stay accountable about their struggles. He is an invaluable resource.

Provide the leadership

- Many young adults lead small groups as well as heading up different aspects of the youth ministry. From overseeing small groups to leading mission trips to different countries—we use them where they are gifted.
- The single adults are awesome and they have time and energy. They can do things with the youth that those with families can not.
- My core planning team is made up of singles in their twenties. They carry the primary responsibility behind me in planning and executing our regular and special events. I don't have any young couples involved.
- One of our most anointed leaders is a young man in his twenties. He really knows how to relate to teens and is always coming up with ideas to get them involved.
- We have had the younger people in their twenties as "teen leaders." They lead worship, sometimes preach, and do altar calls. This has been incredible as the teens feel like they are one of them. They strive to be like these young adults.

Be the connection

- Our young adults have more time to "call" teens and hang out with them. They can share more of the "I remember what it's like" stories, and the kids listen because the age difference is minimal.

- College-agers tend to have more time to spend time with teens, hang out, talk, etc. Our teens will often turn to our single young adults when life gets hard or confusing.

- Each week the teens look forward to the young adults being at youth group. One of the main reasons is they motivate the teens by participating in all the activities with them. They encourage the youth and are their number-one cheerleaders.

- Many of our leaders on our outreach night fall into this category. The teens love their enthusiasm and freshness.

- The twenty-somethings have helped bridge the generational gap of teenager to thirty-something. The youth have seen good examples of how to be a young adult while loving and serving God.

CAN YOU SEE YOURSELF IN THIS PICTURE?

Can you see where you could fully engage in reaching teens? Of course, you will affect them just with the life you live. But you could fully leverage the opportunity you have and leave a legacy. What if you went beyond just making a living and determined to make a difference?

Yes, it's easy to hang out with all your sophisticated friends and do the all things that young couples do. But those teens could be our younger brothers and sisters—and they so often ache in silence.

There is even a self-serving reason to get fully involved in bringing them to Christ. Think about it. They will always be there, following you for the rest of your life. Since there are a lot more of them than members of your own age group, they will determine the society you live in and the culture your kids grow up in.

Go beg your youth leader or youth pastor for an assignment. Go insist that he give you a worthy place to serve. Tell him or her of your determination to impart your love for God to this new generation. The teens need you. The youth pastor needs you. God needs you—now. Choose now one or all of these means of deployment. Don't even finish this book before you decide. Think now. Pray now. Log on to **www.battlecry.com** to enlist as a prayer warrior and tell how you are going to help rescue teenage America.

O God, forgive me for my inaction in the past. Guide me as I take steps to use my influence, sacrifice, and money to rescue this generation. I am disgusted with my own self-justified self-centeredness, and I repent. Use me as a warrior in this battle for the precious souls in this young generation. In Jesus' name I pray. Amen.

v-day is coming

The nation gasped. We couldn't believe our eyes. Unfolding right there on TV was the most horrific violence imaginable. We saw police and firefighters attempting rescues amidst bloodied, lifeless bodies. We watched the wounded struggling to survive.

Who could do such a thing? How could they not care about fellow human beings and their grieving families? Nothing like this had ever happened in our nation, and we would never forget that moment of so much bloodshed—the teenage blood filling our screens on the morning of April 19, 1999.

Did you think I was referring to 9/11? The massacre at Columbine High School bears a striking resemblance to the terrorist attack of September 11, 2001. We were hit by terrorists on both occasions. In both cases, our resolve stiffened. In both cases, our awareness of imminent danger was heightened, and our desire to protect those in our charge was inflamed. Sadly, in both cases we have seen many falter in their commitment to ensure that nothing so destructive will ever happen again. *And now it has.*

On March 21, 2005, 16-year-old Jeff Weise of Red Lake, Minnesota, went on a shooting rampage in his home and at the local high school. He killed nine people and wounded seven others before finally turning a gun on himself. Among the victims: his own grandfather. Instantly, news services across the country referred back to that day of teen terror, calling the Red Lake killings the worst school shooting since Columbine.

Weise's reported social isolation and preoccupation with death certainly echo the troubled history of Columbine killers Eric Harris and Dylan Klebold. Weise found fellowship online—in a neo-Nazi chat room, where he shared plans to promote "racial purity" within his native Chippewa tribe. And even when he dropped morbid hints that revealed not only his state of mind but also his intentions, the people around him didn't recognize the danger signals. When Weise spoke of suicide, of shooting people, of shooting up the school . . . nobody thought he really meant it.

Do you see now that our country's teens are in a moral, emotional, and spiritual crisis? Do you hear them screaming for help as they fall prey to attack after relentless attack on their very souls?

While We Were Sleeping

When engaging with terrorists, we have learned that what we don't do is critical. You see, we remained asleep after several embassy bombings, after the first World Trade Center attack in 1993, and after the bombing of the *USS Cole* in 2000. Our country's inaction clearly signaled America's weakness, saying we probably wouldn't respond in a huge way. Our inaction sent a clear signal to our enemy—we lacked the will to fight.

If Columbine and Red Lake serve as dual wake-up calls to the virtue-terrorist agenda for today's teens, what can we learn from our responses to the 9/11 attack that will aid us in our battle for this generation? Consider:

- *Shock* was our first reaction."How could this be?" we all wondered."And how will this change our future?"
- *Empathy* came next. As we saw the faces and heard the stories, our hearts went out to the victims and their families. We felt as if one of our own had been killed.
- *Fear* kicked in then."Suppose more of these atrocities keep happening?" Everybody began watching the terrorist alert colors and training in awareness and emergency response.
- *Anger* followed on the heels of our fear. We raged at the perpetrators."Who did this, and why?" President Bush stood on the rubble of the World Trade Center and declared,"You will soon hear from us!"
- *Action* then became the demand of the masses. Only a few days after the attack, President Bush said our mission was "to smoke them out of their caves, to get them running so we can get them." All of us agreed: Never again in our own backyard ...

Now Is the Time for Action

The pop techno-terrorists are slowly sucking the life out of a whole generation. They mesmerize teens into a state of apathy and program them to exist in a world that makes the media-shapers even wealthier. They steal youthful dreams and potential. They use free speech as an excuse to market whatever appeals to the lower nature. Then, once they make their millions, we honor them as entrepreneurial geniuses and role models.

Here's my point: Hit by a vicious attack on 9/11, we finally woke up to a terrorist threat that had been gradually building steam for at least three decades. We just couldn't keep our eyes closed anymore to the horror and its implications for our future. But the threat to our teens has been building too. In many ways Columbine was our 9/11 for a whole generation. It seems as though our inaction has emboldened the terrorists of virtue. If we did not wake up and take action then, we must move now while we still have an opportunity to do so—before another Columbine, another Red Lake, happens all over again.

This is your wake-up call! Now is the time for all of us to take action! The enemy has been revealed to you; the casualties of this war now have names and faces. The teens of this nation are crying out to you and the cost of inaction is just too high a price to pay. The only way we can lose this conflict is if we choose not to engage in the battle. You can fight this brand of terrorism in your home, your church, your community. Together we are an unstoppable force, so what are you waiting for?

- ☐ Go online at **www.battlecry.com** and enlist today in the Battle Cry Coalition to receive regular e-mail updates on exactly how to pray and stay involved in practical ways of reaching out to this generation.
- ☐ Gather together a group of others who will read through this book with you using the discussion guide in the back. Pray together how each of you can become more involved in rescuing the teens in your church and community.
- ☐ Make sure your church leaders have read this book. Volunteer to help them spread the word.
- ☐ Talk with the youth leaders in your church. Find ways to invest locally or nationally in youth ministries that are making a positive impact on teens. Give of your time, talents, and finances as God directs.

Taking the High Ground

We have a decided advantage over the enemy. While it may seem that they are bigger and better financed, while it appears that they are well-entrenched in our culture and hold much ground, we have something they don't! People, we own the high ground! Together we form an army with the Power of The One: *"We who are many form one body, and each member belongs to all the others"* (Rom. 12:5). *"There is one body and one Spirit—just as you were called to one hope when you were called—one Lord, one faith, one baptism; one God and Father of all, who is over all and through all and in all"* (Eph. 4:4-6). There is no force more unified in heaven or on earth.

We serve under a code of honor. Unity and focus depend on every soldier knowing and agreeing to certain principles which govern their behavior. In the military, everyone—from the Commander-in-Chief to the foot soldier—adheres to the code. God has given us His code in His Word:

"Hate what is evil; cling to what is good. Be devoted to one another . . . Honor one another . . . Never be lacking in zeal, but keep your spiritual fervor . . . Be joyful in hope, patient in affliction, faithful in prayer" (Rom. 12:9-12).

We understand our mission. Our cause brings truth and life; their cause results in lies and death. *"The thief comes only to steal and kill and destroy; I have come that they may have life, and have it to the full"* (John 10:10). *"Then you will know the truth, and the truth will set you free"* (John 8:32). We fight for what is eternal; therefore, every battle we win has exponential results. Every teen we rescue will influence hundreds of others through their friends, their families, and in future generations.

We know our enemy. With this book, we have destroyed one of terrorism's most powerful weapons—the enemy has been revealed. We know now what we are facing and how to resist:

"Be self-controlled and alert. Your enemy the devil prowls around like a roaring lion looking for someone to devour. Resist him, standing firm in the faith" (1 Pet. 5:8-9).

We are equipped for battle. While it is true that the forces waging this spiritual war against the next generation are well-financed (often with our own money) and well-equipped, God's people are well-armed. We have the sword of truth and the shield of faith. We have a General who has promised us that

"... *no weapon forged against you will prevail, and you will refute every tongue that accuses you. This is the heritage of the servants of the LORD* ..." *(Isa. 54:17).*

Our Master and Commander is the Creator of the cosmos. There is nothing He does not know, no power He cannot defeat, no place He is not already present, no resource not at His command. He has absolute authority over all and has given that authority to us (Matt. 28:18). We cannot fail unless we choose not to act. As we mobilize our troops, let us take the words of Romans 8:37 as our banner: "We are more than conquerors." Let us stand together; let us keep focused not on what the enemy has to lose but on what we have to gain. Our future hangs in the balance. Are you ready? Are you willing? It's time to enlist because V-Day is coming!

discussion guide

For Group Discussion or Personal Reflection

discussion guide

How far would you go to save a person's life?
What about an entire generation?

Battle Cry for a Generation calls Christians to take drastic action on behalf of the millions of young people ensnared in today's soul-killing philosophies and perverted media. The Enemy of our souls has breached America's foundation of biblical principles, and every day he pulls more teens into the flames of deception, despair, and destruction.

Now is the time to choose what role you will play in the struggle. As you read this book, either on your own or with a discussion group, the following questions will help you understand the magnitude of the war and find your assignment.

Whether you currently work with America's youth or are wondering how you can help, allow God to speak to you through the message of this book. Don't let another day go by or another life slip away. You can help a dying generation find new life in Christ. You can affect the moral character of our country. You *can* make a difference!

CHAPTER ONE

1. Ron compared the situation facing the next generation to a car on fire with teens trapped inside. How does the current media war against our teens compare in terms of urgency, danger, and need?

2. Ron points out that the largest generation since WW II (71 million) is about to change our world. What is the potential impact of the spiritual health of today's teens on your future?

3. Share your reaction to the following statement: "What you believe by the time you're 13 is what you'll die believing."

4. What would motivate you to take action now to save our young people for Christ?

5. Do you share Ron's sense of "holy urgency?" Why or why not?

CHAPTER TWO

1. What do you know about "the enemy"? Compare how well you know the enemy to how well you know yourself and your sphere of influence. What will you do to increase your knowledge of the enemy so you can sharpen your "battle plan"?

2. Ron presented the "bad news" statistics on the four biggest media influences in a teen's life: TV and movies, music, video games, and the Internet. What did you already know, and what did you learn? Where do you see these statistics reflected in the habits of teens from your community, your church—or your own home?

3. This chapter also reports on the cumulative effect that media content has on a teen. What have you personally observed in teens you know?

4. Christian teens live in the same media-saturated world as the rest of their generation. Is the effect different for the teens who attend your church as opposed to those who don't attend church? If so, how? If not, why not?

5. Given the statistics in this book, what action can you take to improve the chances of rescuing this generation?

CHAPTER THREE

1. Describe how you may have "retreated" from the battle for saving today's youth.

2. How would you characterize your current commitment as a Christian? Did you join a club or enlist in an army? Explain.

3. Take a moment to compare the peacetime vs. wartime mentality lists. Which best characterizes your church? How does that fit where you are right now?

4. "Our joy as a soldier is to find our Commander's assignment and throw our lives into embracing Him and His mission for us." How can we know God's assignment for each of us? What is God's assignment for you?

5. What, if anything, holds you back from full-fledged enlistment in God's Army?

CHAPTER FOUR

1. Ron compares the destructive effects of the media's sexualization of teens to the unhealthy exposure to cigarette smoke. How has this infiltration of sensual media programs affected your community?

2. A study by the RAND corporation indicates that the still-developing teenage brain cannot protect itself against the effects of pornographic stimuli. Teens clearly need adult input and protection. What will you do to offer this protection to the teens in your life?

3. Family Safe Media reports that "90 percent of eight to sixteen year olds have viewed porn online (most while doing homework)." Whether you have kids, would like to have kids in the future, or simply babysit for friends, what precautions would you take to prevent this from happening in the home?

4. According to Dr. May Laydon in testimony given to the U.S. Senate, pornographic visual images cause addictive "brain sabotage." What are the long-term implications for today's visually oriented teen generation?

5. The teen game "Snap" uses Jelly Bracelets to invite future hook-ups. What are you doing to stay aware of teen "codes" for sexual behavior? How will you use that knowledge to challenge teens you know to protect their sexual purity?

CHAPTER FIVE

1. In this chapter, Ron mentions a popular twist on the Golden Rule: "He who has the gold, rules!" What can Christians do to counteract this influence?

2. Today's teenagers, including teens in your church, are showing signs of buying into today's values. How can you encourage struggling parents to teach biblical values to and set biblical standards for their children?

3. Ron cites a National Institute of Mental Health study that measures the effect that viewing pornography has on key brain chemicals, fusing conscious sexual arousal with the unconscious "fight" (anger, hostility) and "flight" (fear, shame) emotions. How does this connect to cases of sexual dysfunction and abuse?

4. Chap Clark concludes, in his study of high school students, that teens use sex as a "temporary salve for the pain and loneliness resulting from abandonment." Tell about a lonely teen you know. What can you and your church do to help today's suffering teens?

5. Teens who have experimented with Internet pornography may have already left your church. How can you help them return? Likewise, how can you help teens who currently attend your church resist the temptations of online porn?

CHAPTER SIX

1. Ron says "We can't win a culture war just by fighting the evil forces ...we can't argue or debate ...we must capture the hearts of young people." What does it mean, in practical terms, to capture a young heart in this way?

2. Ron gives four steps for a counterinvasion. Next to each step, suggest one tactic for reaching that goal either at home or at church, or in your community:
   a. Capture their hearts.
   b. Establish a beachhead.
   c. Develop *esprit de corps*.
   d. Enter the fight.

3. Why is it important for us to speak with a unified voice? What can you do, both personally and as a church, to help give strength to that voice?

4. To win this war, we will need to go after the kids no one else wants. How can you help your church prepare for that kind of outreach?

5. Read again The Teenage Bill of Rights in this chapter. What parts of this document do you find challenging in your own life? How can you support teens who are willing to take up this challenge?

CHAPTER SEVEN

1. Ron suggests that our church must become a place of healing for the brokenhearted. What are some practical examples of that happening in your church already? What would need to change to make this happen church-wide?

2. Do you see teens as a vital part of your church? Why or why not? How can you help encourage a more passionate pursuit of youth in your church?

3. Contact your church treasurer for an estimate of how much of the annual budget is spent on the youth. What does this amount say about your church's commitment to youth?

4. In the surveys for youth pastors, what quote surprised you the most? How can you do more to encourage your youth pastor?

5. How has your view of youth ministry changed since starting this book?

CHAPTER EIGHT

1. Step into the shoes of your youth pastor for a moment. What more would you need to "lead like a general in a destiny-based ministry"?

2. Ron says that youth ministries must become vision driven and not just activity driven. How would you describe the current youth ministry in your church? In what ways could your youth leaders best share their vision with the rest of your church membership?

3. How can *you* help the members of your church catch the youth pastor's vision for ministry?

4. Think of the church in your town with the largest youth ministry. Would you say they are vision or activity oriented? Why?

5. What might be holding back your youth leaders from reaching teens more effectively? What can you do to help improve the situation?

CHAPTER NINE

1. Ron suggests three "drastic measures" parents must take to save their own sons and daughters from the effects of today's media. Which of these do you already practice in your home? Which ones will you consider starting in your home?

2. Think of a time when you clearly supported a child's dreams. How much time, money, and other resources did you commit to this support? How can those same resources now be applied to saving this generation?

3. How involved are parents of teens in your church? What could be done both by church staff and by parents to get more parents involved?

4. Ron encourages all of us to take responsibility for the sons and daughters of America. What will that look like for you?

5. There are many parents of teens who are either unable or unwilling to support their kids. How can adults of all ages, parents or not, help to fill the gap?

CHAPTER TEN

1. Ron asks all Christian men to use their influence and finances to protect this generation. How do you see the men of your church responding to this call? What specifically can you do to respond?

2. Think of every businessman that you know. How might you get them involved with your church's youth ministry?

3. Ron also calls upon the senior adults to help reach this generation of teens. What are some unique contributions this group can make? List three ways your church could help bring these two groups together this year.

        a. _____

        b. _____

        c. _____

4. What are some of the advantages that twenty-somethings have when working with teens? How can your church facilitate interaction between your college/career-aged members and your teen members?

5. After visiting www.battlecry.com, discuss your plan to show your support for this historic national mission. Ask your small group to be a source of accountability for you in following through with your plan.

The Word at Work Around the World

*W*hat would you do if you wanted to share God's love with children on the streets of your city? That's the dilemma David C. Cook faced in 1870's Chicago. His answer was to create literature that would capture children's hearts.

Out of those humble beginnings grew a worldwide ministry that has used literature to proclaim God's love and disciple generation after generation. Cook Communications Ministries is committed to personal discipleship—to helping people of all ages learn God's Word, embrace His salvation, walk in His ways, and minister in His name.

Faith Kidz, RiverOak, Honor, Life Journey, Victor, NextGen . . . every time you purchase a book produced by Cook Communications Ministries, you not only meet a vital personal need in your life or in the life of someone you love, but you're also a part of ministering to José in Colombia, Humberto in Chile, Gousa in India, or Lidiane in Brazil. You help make it possible for a pastor in China, a child in Peru, or a mother in West Africa to enjoy a life-changing book. And because you helped, children and adults around the world are learning God's Word and walking in His ways.

Thank you for your partnership in helping to disciple the world. May God bless you with the power of His Word in your life.

For more information about our international ministries, visit www.ccmi.org.

TEEN MANIA
MINISTRIES

Teen Mania is fighting for today's teens.

Teen Mania's heartbeat is to provoke a young generation to passionately pursue Jesus Christ and to take His life-giving message to the ends of the earth.

Founded in 1986 by Ron Luce, Teen Mania reaches teens through several primary outreaches:

Events

Held in approximately 30 cities across North America each year, Acquire the Fire events create an environment where teens' hearts are captured by God, and biblical truths are imparted through high-impact multimedia, live drama, music and teaching.

www.battlecry.com
(click on "Events")

Mission Trips

Global Expeditions is committed to bringing the Truth of Jesus Christ to the countless thousands around the world who are in desperate need of His love. Teens and leaders travel the world with Global Expeditions and bring the message of hope to the hopeless. Since its inception in 1986, Teen Mania has taken more than 40,000 teens around the world and documented over one million people who have committed their lives to Christ as a result.

www.globalexpeditions.com

Internship

The Honor Academy gives high school graduates an opportunity to impact the world for Christ while developing the character and leadership skills they need for life-long success. Interns are actively involved in all the ministries of Teen Mania. The scope of the program is extensive and includes classroom instruction, practical hands-on experience, and life-transforming events.

www.honoracademy.com

Media

The Center of Creative Media trains young innovators to connect their culture with the message of the gospel. CCM interns not only receive training from industry experts, they are also actively involved in producing media for live events, the Internet and broadcast. The Acquire the Fire TV show attracts approximately 400,000 viewers each week across North America, and many more in over 200 nations around the world.

www.centerforcreativemedia.com

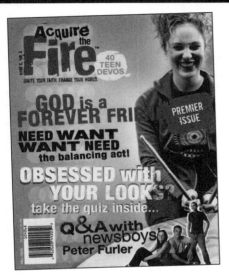
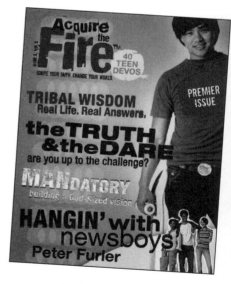